Spelling for Writers

Mary Jo Fresch • Aileen Wheaton

Teacher's Edition
Grade 2

GReaT S✣uRCe®
EDUCATION GROUP
A Division of Houghton Mifflin Company

Mary Jo Fresch previously taught third grade and Adult Literacy classes. She taught children's literature and literacy courses in teacher education programs in Ohio, Nebraska, and Melbourne, Australia. She received her Ph.D. from The Ohio State University, where she is currently an Associate Professor in the College of Education. She resides in Dublin, Ohio, with her husband, Hank. She has two children, Michael and Angela (and son-in-law Nathan Thompson).

Aileen Ford Wheaton previously was a primary and intermediate elementary classroom teacher. After years in the classroom, Aileen became a district Literacy Intervention Specialist. She also taught preschool, adult literacy classes, G.E.D., and English as a Second Language. A native of North Dakota, Aileen currently resides in Columbus, Ohio with her husband, Jim. She has two sons, Michael and Andrew (and daughter-in-law Katie).

Printed in the United States of America

International Standard Book Number: 0-669-51749-6

1 2 3 4 5 6 7 8 9 10 – BA – 10 09 08 07 06 05

Contents

Lessons

Introducing

Spelling for Writers

Spelling for Writers provides a manageable way for students to explore the English language; develop numerous strategies; develop their ability to look at, listen to, and think about words; and, finally, to extend that learning into becoming fluent writers. The title of this program, *Spelling for Writers*, tells it all. We no longer assign spelling, we teach children how to wonder about the language, learn its features, and become word historians.

In *Spelling for Writers*, students will

- study words "from the inside out" and notice patterns.

- understand where words come from and why they are spelled the way they are.

- transfer knowledge of word patterns from their spelling lists to their writing.

- learn proofreading techniques that are applicable to all writing.

In *Spelling for Writers*, teachers will have

- easy-to-follow weekly lessons.

- an organized way to manage individualized word lists.

- built-in differentiated instruction.

- support from the Teacher's Edition, Transparencies, Posters, and CD-ROM.

- flexibility in deciding how the program best meets their students' needs.

Annotated Lesson

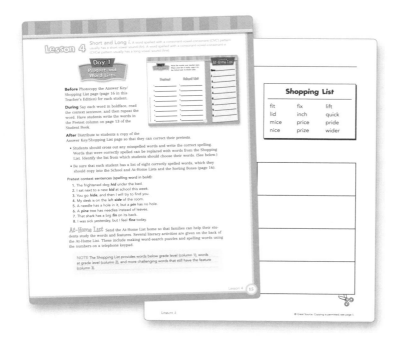

Day 1 includes a teacher-directed pretest. Students create their own word lists for study by replacing correctly spelled words with Shopping List words. This list offers students additional at-grade-level words or, for students needing differentiated instruction, words below or above grade level. Students copy the final list onto the School and At-Home Lists in the Student Book. The At-Home List tears out of the Student Book. On the back is the Dear Families letter that provides weekly communication with students' families.

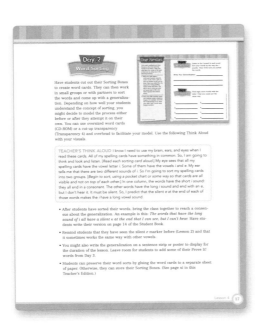

Day 2 is hands-on and active. Teachers use the Teacher's Think Aloud and large word cards (from the CD-ROM), or a cut-up transparency (from the Transparencies) to model how to sort the words. Eventually, students take over the sorting themselves. Students collaboratively form a generalization that states what spelling pattern makes the words similar or different. The focus of word sorting is for students to compare and contrast words in order to observe dependable spelling features.

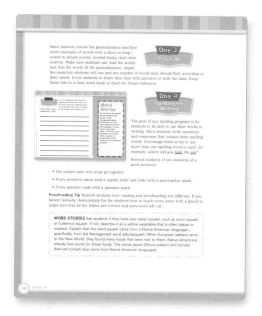

Days 3-4 Students find words in sources outside the program that prove the generalization. Discussion and sharing of the words expands students' word knowledge. As students become more aware of a particular feature, they begin to see it and hear it everywhere!

Students show what they know about the word feature in a writing assignment. Specific proofreading tips help students become more accurate writers.

The word history feature encourages a curiosity about language. Once students get hooked, they will want to know where every word came from!

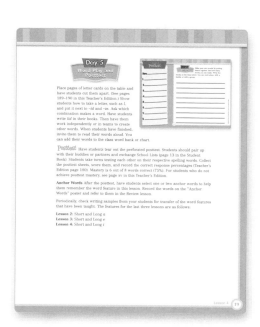

Day 5 The posttest shows whether students understand the word feature they have studied. The posttest tears out of the Student Book for convenience.

The word play activities are appropriate for independent, paired, or small group work. They can be used to bring the concept to closure or for review before the posttest.

5-Day Plan

Day of the Week	Purpose	What the teacher does	What the students do
Day 1 **Pretest and Word Lists** *15-20 minutes*	Assess current level of knowledge of word feature. Establish a word list for the week.	Orally presents words in context sentences. Hands out answer keys for students to self-correct their pretests. Circulates, providing guidance as students self-select words from the Shopping List.	Take pretest. Proofread own attempts. Highlight incorrect attempts. Select words from Shopping List to replace any correctly spelled words. Copy words onto the School List and At-Home List. Fill in Sorting Boxes. Take the At-Home List home!
Day 2 **Word Sorting** *15-20 minutes*	Identify common sound and spelling patterns and sort the words into groups with similar word features.	Prepares master set of Sorting Boxes. Uses cards in pocket chart or an overhead transparency to model sorting for the group. Brings group to consensus on generalization related to the word features. Records and displays the generalizations.	Cut apart Sorting Boxes. Sort words into categories that make sense. Write a generalization about the words in the Student Book. Share discoveries during whole-class discussion.

Day of the Week	Purpose	What the teacher does	What the students do
Day 3 **Prove It!** *5 minutes of initial instruction, independent search during other literacy work, 10 minutes to share words*	Prove the generalization and apply it to a larger of pool of words in the "real world."	Revisits generalization. Gives direction for words search (i.e., where students will hunt for more words that are similar to the pattern). Discusses words that fit the pattern and those that do not.	Find words that are similar to this week's pattern. Students may work independently or collaboratively. Record words in the Student Book.
Day 4 **Spelling for Writing** *5 minutes of instruction, independent writing during other literacy work*	Write words in context and practice proofreading skills.	Assigns the writing assignment and teaches the proofreading tip.	Create written text in the Student Book using this week's words. Proofread writing.
Day 5 **Word Play** **and Posttest** *10 minutes*	Review words through word play. Assess knowledge of the feature.	Supervises posttest given by spelling buddies or administers posttest. Collects and grades the posttest. Looks for 75% mastery. Returns to generalization with students to select "anchor" words to use to remember the spelling feature.	Use Student Book for word play. Take the posttest.

Variation for 3-day plan:

Day 1 Pretest and Word Sort

Day 2 Prove It! and Spelling for Writing

Day 3 Word Play and Posttest

Classroom Management

Fitting Spelling for Writers into Literacy Instruction

Instructional settings and needs vary across classrooms. However, *Spelling for Writers* is flexible enough to use in any classroom setting.

Fitting Spelling for Writers into the Language Arts Class *Spelling for Writers* fits with other literacy instruction because a student's word knowledge is essential in all areas of literacy – reading, writing, listening, and speaking. *Spelling for Writers* offers teachers another opportunity to discuss how we can read and write words. The writing activity can easily be carried over to writing workshop, as many of the *Spelling for Writing* ideas are good "starters" that could be continued in workshop time. The Four Blocks® approach includes a word analysis component, and the sorting and word play days are compatible with the philosophy of that program. Word hunts and word histories could become a center.

Flexible Scheduling *Spelling for Writers* is set up as a five-day routine. Many teachers do their spelling lessons from Monday through Friday; however, the authors recommend starting on Tuesday or Wednesday and going into the next week so that families have the weekend to work on the activities in the Dear Families letter. The lessons can be adapted in the following ways:

- Combine activities to form a three-day routine (see page ix).
- The word hunt activity on Day 3 and the writing activity on Day 4 can be handled by the students once they have direction from the teacher. Therefore, they can be used any time during the literacy instruction, as homework assignments, or as on-going activities.
- Limit the time allotted for certain activities, such as the word hunt, writing, and word play.

Customizing the Lists

Day 1 includes a pretest that is teacher directed, followed by the students' involvement in creating a word list for study. How this list is developed can vary depending on the instructional needs. The intent is for students to self-select, but in particular classrooms or at particular times of the year, the teacher may choose to be more directive in influencing student lists. Whichever way the lists are developed, all students will be examining the same word feature.

Whole Class Use the pretest words for everyone and work only with those words throughout the cycle of activities, all the way through the teacher-administered posttest. For teachers new to the program, this is a good way to manage the lessons at the beginning of the year while they and the students become familiar with *Spelling for Writers* and each other. Once teachers and students are comfortable with the program, they can begin to incorporate elements of customization.

Small Groups Teachers who already manage several reading groups for literacy instruction can use those same groups for spelling instruction. Each group can work with the teacher to determine the word list for the lesson. At the end of the week, the teacher administers the posttest to each group.

Individuals *Spelling for Writers* will be most effective if each student has a customized list. Student motivation is a powerful learning tool, and when students feel ownership and in control of their words, they are motivated to learn. Teachers can advise students which section of the Shopping List to use (below, on, or above grade level), based on very specific knowledge of how students are doing in spelling or in accordance with the students' reading levels. Spelling buddies can use each other's School List to test each other. Teachers then collect and grade the posttests.

Managing the Word Cards

One of the challenges of word sorting is how to handle the sorting boxes, or word cards.

Making the Word Cards

- Photocopy the Answer Key/Shopping List page for students each week. When their lists are ready, have them copy the words into the boxes. This can be a homework assignment if students have filled in their At-Home List.

- Photocopy the copy master from the Transparencies and Copy Master folder for each student. Only the pretest words are on this sheet.

- Use the CD-ROM to produce word cards for students or large word cards to use when modeling a word sort for the class.

Using the Word Cards

- Once students have made their final sorts, they can preserve them by taping or gluing the word cards to a sheet of paper. Slip the paper inside the back cover of the Student Book for the week or keep all the sorts in a separate spelling folder.

- To keep the cards available for re-use, have students store the cards (see below).

- Word cards can be kept in a word study center for students to use in their free time. They can also be sent home for further practice.

Storing the Word Cards

- Store the cards in envelopes or resealable plastic bags. Label each envelope or bag with the lesson number. A class set of envelopes or bags can be stored in the *Spelling for Writers* box or in a file box in the word study center.

- Use a paper clip to keep the cards together. Attach the word cards to the inside back cover of the Student Book.

- Instead of storing the word cards, new word cards can be printed out as needed from the CD-ROM.

How the Words Were Chosen

Pretest Words

Using several research based word lists, the pretest words were selected from lists used by nearly every research-based spelling series. These include lists that analyzed the highly frequent reading and writing words for particular grade levels. The word lists in the early years begin with rime patterns, proven to be the highest occurring primary words in students' reading and writing. Lists used as a resource for this key component to the lessons were Dale and O'Rourke's *Living Word Vocabulary* (1976), Greene's *New Iowa Spelling Scale* (1961), Hanna, Hanna, Hodges and Rudorf's *Phoneme-grapheme Correspondences as Cues to Spelling Improvement* (1966), Henderson's *Teaching Spelling* (1990), Dolch's *High-Frequency Sight Words List* (1936), and Wylie and Durrell's *37 phonograms* (1970). Additionally, the linguistic research that focuses on the developmentally appropriate continuum for learning to spell guided the selection of the grade level features. The work of Read (1971), Henderson (1977, 1990), Templeton (1989), and Schlagal (1992) provided the match between grade levels and the features on which the lessons focus. Once the features and grade levels were matched, the researched lists were used to select grade level words that would serve as excellent models for the students to work with and observe the spelling features. At the primary grades, lists of 6-8 words were devised. At the upper elementary grades, lists of 12 words were created. These word lists provide the students opportunity to carefully examine patterns so that they get into how the patterns sound and are spelled. Only then can they generalize their new learning to other words they choose to write. These numbers are also manageable for the sorting day and to provide the teacher with manageable numbers for meeting individual needs.

Shopping List Words

Using the same careful selection as in the pretest words, additional words at each grade level were selected. Should individualization be needed, students can select from below- or above-grade-level words. This shows students the wide range of words using the same pattern. It also permits a community of learning to occur: All students are looking at the exact same pattern, even though they are using words appropriate to their reading and writing level.

Repetition of Words

Occasionally teachers may notice a word being used more than once in a school year for more than one feature. By examining a word in more than one way, we reinforce to students that it is about developing strategies for becoming a better speller—not about memorizing a word for the posttest. Often, the second time a student comes to a word, he or she will remember it in a different way. This provides another dependable resource for students: There are multiple ways to look at and remember the spellings of words.

Frequently Asked Questions

What is a word feature? A word feature is a spelling pattern that can be observed across a number of English words. The feature helps us both read and write a word. There are many dependable features of our language that we can help students learn to provide power to their reading and writing. For example, when we see English words that are Consonant, Vowel, Consonant (CVC), we know that the vowel has a short sound. This feature, then, is a short vowel sound.

What is a generalization? A generalization is a statement about the feature that a group of words share. *Spelling for Writers* selects the spelling features that have the broadest application in English words and will help develop dependable strategies for students when writing independently. Establishing the generalization of the spelling feature is a way for students to organize their thinking about words.

Why is word sorting important? Sorting is the hands-on, active learning element of *Spelling for Writers*. The sorting activity gives students a way "into" words. It provides a concrete, manipulative way to learn new words. Because they talk about, listen to, look at, and analyze words, students learn more about how to spell a large number of words.

Why can't students just memorize the words? A memorization model limits students to using only the correct spelling and usage of words they can remember. Research demonstrates that memorization can disempower some learners who need a variety of strategies available to them. Strategies that broaden a student's understanding of the language provide multiple opportunities for students to expand their knowledge

How is the instruction in *Spelling for Writers* differentiated? The philosophy of *Spelling for Writers* has been applied to a wide range of learners. Students study the same feature but have individualized lists because the Shopping List offers additional words below, at, and above grade level. Support is provided for every learner in the following ways: The teacher can adjust the number of words, the teacher or students can select the difficulty of words, and students can work with a knowledgeable peer.

How does *Spelling for Writers* work with English Learners? *Spelling for Writers* helps English Learners by helping them understand how English works. Memorizing words does not help these learners apply their knowledge outside the posttest. *Spelling for Writers* helps them see the patterns and discover ways to make connections across a large number of words. Pretest context sentences are provided to help students understand the words tested; conversations during the sorting and word play help students with their speaking and listening vocabulary.

Is it OK for students to give each other the posttest? The question of "cheating" sometimes comes up in the context of buddy situations. Since students understand the focus is on word features rather than whole words, the stigma of being a "master" of a certain number of words is removed. Instead, they are part of a community of learners working to master a spelling feature and its many applications in the English language.

Assessment in *Spelling for Writers*

Formal Weekly Tests

Pretest Each lesson begins with a teacher-directed pretest, given through context sentences. Students record the words in the Student Book. Teachers have the option of correcting the test themselves, but the power of *Spelling for Writers* lies in the empowerment of students and their ability to take control of their learning. Students check the words against the Answer Key. They copy the correct spelling of misspelled words from the Answer Key, and they replace correctly spelled words with Shopping List words.

The pretest is the starting point for studying a word feature. It shows what students know about the word feature, even though the feature is not "announced" at the time of the pretest. Students will be encouraged to discover it the next day. However, once they realize how the lists are organized, many students will begin to predict what the feature is as they take the pretest.

Posttest The purpose of the posttest is to see how well students have learned the word feature they studied during the week. If students have customized their lists, the posttest will show whether they can generalize the feature. The teacher can give the posttest to the whole class or to small groups, or spelling buddies can give the test to each other. Record posttest scores in the class record chart on Teacher's Edition page 180.

Periodic Developmental Assessment

Review Because *Spelling for Writers* focuses on helping students understand, learn, and apply the spelling features in English, the review weeks focus, once again, on the spelling features. Following each lesson's posttest, the teacher and students collaboratively establish a couple of anchor words and record them on the "Anchor Words" poster. These are the words that students can refer to when applying the knowledge learned during the lessons. When giving the pretest for the review weeks, teachers can once again observe how students are applying their knowledge. There are three ways the teacher may give this pretest:

- The teacher can announce the feature and ask the students to write a word that contains that features. ("Write a word that is a compound word.")

- The teacher can refer to the anchor word. ("When we studied compound words, we selected *wristwatch* as an anchor word to help us remember that feature. What is another compound word?")

- The teacher can give the students options of words she or he has chosen from the previous lessons. ("Which of these words is compound? Listen as I say three words— *Tuesday, wristwatch, happily*. Write the compound word.").

For any words students write correctly, they should be asked to go back to their word hunt for that week and find a word they would like to add to their list to learn to spell. Again, the teacher may choose words for the students to select from by looking back at the posttest, or selecting from the CD-ROM. This review week provides one more opportunity for the students to learn the feature and to understand they are not memorizing words; rather, they are learning how the English language works so that they develop dependable strategies for application to writing.

Benchmark Assessment *Spelling for Writers* provides assessment opportunities three times across every grade level. Specifically, these benchmark assessments allow the teacher to observe the features students already know that will be taught in the coming year. This will help with differentiated instruction for all types of learners. By repeating the assessment mid-year and end of the year, the teacher has concrete evidence of growth. This provides documentation to parents, schools, and other educators working with the students. Since the same words are used each time, the teacher can directly observe how the students' strategies are changing and improving.

Classroom Writing The real "test" of whether students understand the generalizations is in their writing. As students learn more word features, teachers should hold them accountable for using the features in their writing. At the end of every three lessons in *Spelling for Writers*, there is a reminder to the teacher to check students' writing for accurate use of recently learned word features.

Grading the Posttest and Reteaching

On the posttest, 6 correctly spelled words out of 8 is considered mastery of the feature. If students score below that level, try the reteaching activities listed below.

Number Correct	8	7	6	5	4	3	2	1
Percentage	100%	87.5%	75%	62.5%	50%	37.5%	20%	12.5%

Reteaching the Word Feature Students who do not understand the word feature can be helped with the following suggestions:

- Find out what the student was thinking when he or she made an attempt at writing a word. Ask questions such as the following:
  - What were you hearing and thinking about as you wrote this word?
  - What other words like this do you know?
  - How might you remember how this spelling pattern sounds and looks?
  - Let's try writing this again. You listen as I say it, then I want you to proofread what you wrote and see if you it looks like the word I said.

- Keep a set of word cards available. Have the student sort the words and explain the sort to you. Then, have the student do the sort repeatedly. Sorting speed is not competition between students; rather, an individual can do timed sorts to beat his or her own record. Speed sorting leads to automaticity, which in turn leads to more fluent reading and writing.

Spelling for Writers Scope and Sequence

Word Feature	Grade 1	Grade 2	Grade 3	Grade 4	Grade 5	Grade 6
Vowels						
Short	x	x	x	x	x	x
In word families	x	x	x			
In closed syllable		x	x	x	x	x
In multisyllabic words		•	x	x	x	x
Long	x	x	x	x	x	x
/e/ marker	•	x	x	x		
Vowel sound of /y/		•	x	x	x	x
In silent letter patterns		•	x	x	x	x
R-controlled			•	x	x	x
More complex				•	x	x
Complex patterns			•	x	x	x
Diphthongs			•	x	x	x
Alternations				•	x	x
Consonants						
Alphabet	x					
Initial	x	x				
Final	x	x				
Final *k, ck*		•	x			
Within words	x	x				
Blends	•	x	x	x		
Digraphs	•	x	x		x	x
Preconsonant nasals		•	x	x	x	
Soft and hard sound of /c/ and /g/		•	x			
Patterns *qu, ph, mb*		•	x			
Silent patterns		•	x	x		x
Doubling before adding endings			•	x	x	
Doubling at syllable juncture				•		x
Alternations						•
Meaning Influences						
Prefixes			•	x	x	x
Absorbed/Assimilated					•	x
Greek/Latin					•	x
Numerical						•
Suffixes			•	x	x	x
Endings *-tion, -sion, -cian*					•	x
-ible, -able						•
-al, -el, -le						•
Plurals		•	x	x	x	x
Plural irregular forms			•	x	x	x
Past tense		•	x	x		
Past tense irregular forms			•	x		
Comparatives			•	x	x	x
Superlatives			•	x	x	x
Greek/Latin					•	x
Homonyms			•	x		
Derivations and relations				•	x	x
Compound words			•	x	x	x
Contractions				•	x	
Dictionary terms				•	x	x
Possessives					•	x
Words from other languages					•	
Synonyms/Antonyms					•	x
Homographs					•	
Greek/Latin roots					•	x
Eponyms					•	x
Portmanteau words					•	
Acronyms					•	
Idioms						•
Onomatopoeia						•

• introduction
x review

Days 1-2

Word Lists

Days 1-2
Word Lists

Write the words your teacher says.

Benchmark Assessment

1._____   11._____
2._____   12._____
3._____   13._____
4._____   14._____
5._____   15._____
6._____   16._____
7._____   17._____
8._____   18._____
9._____   19._____
10._____   20._____

Dear Families,

This week your child will be given a benchmark spelling assessment. This assessment is a tool to gain insight into your child's current and developing knowledge about spelling. Information from the benchmark assessments will allow for classroom instruction that builds on what your child already knows. Your child will take the same benchmark assessment in the middle of the year and again at the end of the year. By looking at the three benchmarks, your child's growth and development will be evident and will inform next year's teacher about this year's progress.

Weekly pretests and posttests will monitor your child's progress in learning each of the word features (for example, vowel patterns, plurals, past tense, consonant blends). Nevertheless, the true "test" of spelling is in your child's writing.

Before Have students locate page 1 in the Student Book on which they will record the spelling words. Over the next five days, you will establish a benchmark for each student. This benchmark assessment will be repeated in the middle of the year and again at the end, allowing you to show each student's growth. There are no standards for mastery in the benchmark assessments. Rather, they are informative pieces for instructional planning.

During Say each word in boldface (page 2) aloud. The word features are identified in parentheses for your information. These words were specifically chosen because they represent grade-level words for a given feature. If you substitute other words in this lesson, use the same words in the other benchmark assessments. It is recommended that this assessment be administered over two to five days, in short intervals, in order to best meet the needs of your students and to avoid student fatigue. On Days 3–5, if the assessment is still ongoing, students can continue with the other activities after you administer a small portion of the assessment.

After Interpret students' responses, analyzing first their successes in spelling a word that meets the word feature criterion and then taking a hard look at where they may have miscued, perhaps recalling a different word feature and misapplying it. For example, if a student spells *folded* as "fodid," you can gain several distinct insights. The student has good knowledge of long vowels. He or she knows about and can hear beginning and final consonants. However, the student's operating knowledge of *ed* and *ld* are not developed as independent strategies. The student is relying on phonemic strategies that represent an auditory approach. Based on these insights, you would want to use the student's auditory skills to build his or her visual skills.

We suggest you do not mark in the Student Book. A record sheet is provided (see page 179 in this Teacher's Edition). This records the features and allows you to document growth for each student. It is important for students not to see the markings, so simply transfer any attempts to the record sheet. This reinforces the understanding that *Spelling for Writers* developmentally supports the spelling strategies that students bring to their writing, rather than focusing on mastery of whole words. As you will notice, the students' profile easily documents growth.

Benchmark Assessment This is the first of three Benchmark Assessments. The Benchmark Assessments provide a record of students' spelling from this year and can be noted in a portfolio and passed along to next year's teachers.

1. **late** (short and long vowel *a*)
2. **yes** (short and long vowel *e*)
3. **big** (short and long vowel *i*)
4. **toe** (short and long vowel *o*)
5. **use** (short and long vowel *u*)
6. **try** (long vowel *y*)
7. **man** (short vowels *a, i*)
8. **mop** (short vowels *e, o*)
9. **dust** (short vowel *u*, long vowel *y*)
10. **keep** (long vowels *a, e, o*)
11. **ice** (long vowels *i, u*)
12. **child** (digraphs)
13. **free** (consonants blends)
14. **kick** (final consonants)

15. **stars** (plural *-s*)
16. **foxes** (plural *-es*)
17. **men** (irregular plurals)
18. **know** (silent consonant patterns)
19. **high** (silent vowel patterns)
20. **rain** (silent vowel patterns)
21. **told** (irregular past tense)
22. **wrapped** (past tense *-ed*)
23. **thank** (preconsonant nasals)
24. **apple** (short and long vowel *a*)
25. **letter** (short and long vowel *e*)
26. **inside** (short and long vowel *i*)
27. **opening** (short and long vowel *o*)
28. **cuter** (short and long vowel *u*)

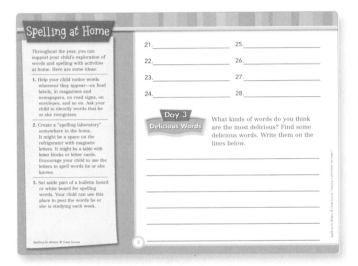

Letter to the Families

Students may carefully remove the perforated section of page 1 in the Student Book and take it home to share with their families. It includes a note to families explaining the benchmark assessments and how they will be used to shape instruction. On the back of this note are several At-Home activities that families can use to support their students' learning. These activities include noticing words in environmental print, creating a "spelling laboratory" where students can manipulate letters to form words, and making a spelling board where students can display their words each week.

Day 3
Delicious Words

After students have completed today's benchmark assessment, tell them that they are going to go on a word hunt. Tell them that they will look for words they would call "delicious"—words that are fun, descriptive, or vivid; words that help them imagine how something looks, feels, tastes, smells, or sounds. For example, if you were reading *Charlotte's Web* to your class, you might note wonderful phrases like "a barn that is perfumed with rotten egg" or "he felt radiant and happy." Talk with students about words that could make their writing come alive, like *perfumed* or *radiant*. Provide appropriate materials for the word hunt, such as picture books and children's magazines. Students should write their words on page 2 of the Student Book. Keep an on-going list on the "Delicious Words" poster as a resource of terrific words for students to use in their writing.

Day 4
Spelling for Writing

After students have completed today's benchmark assessment, review the instructions for the writing activity. Make sure students understand what a headline is—the title for a newspaper story. A headline uses just a few words to tell the main idea of the story. Students may work in pairs to brainstorm events that have happened recently or are coming up at school. Then they can work independently to write their headlines.

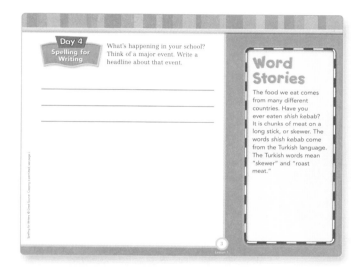

Proofreading Tip Explain to students that proofreading is a special kind of reading that writers do to make sure that their writing has no errors. Proofreading must be done slowly and carefully. Show students how to touch a pencil point to each word so that their eyes will focus on only one word at a time.

Word Stories On Student Book page 3, students are asked if they have ever eaten shish kebab. Traditionally, Turkish shish kebab features lamb. Then ask students if they know two other food words that come from the Turkish language: *yogurt* and *pilaf*. Yogurt is a custard-like food made from milk and often flavored with fruit. Pilaf (Turkish *pilav*) is a rice dish with meat and/or vegetables. On Student Book page 4, students are asked to find out some information about a food that they like to eat. Encourage the discovery of different words associated with the food, such as the ingredients, the process used to make it (e.g., broil, blend, whip), and the history of the name itself.

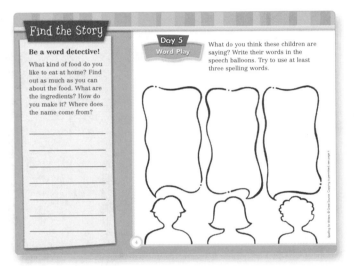

After students have completed today's benchmark assessment, have them turn to page 4 of the Student Book. Make sure they understand that the speech balloons are for the words spoken by the people in the picture. Ask them to look carefully at the cartoon and think about what each person might be saying.

Lesson 2

Short and Long a. A word spelled with a consonant-vowel-consonant (CVC) pattern usually has a short vowel sound (c*a*p). A word spelled with a consonant-vowel-consonant-e (CVCe) pattern usually has a long vowel sound (c*a*pe).

Day 1
Pretest and Word Lists

Before Photocopy the Answer Key/ Shopping List page (page 6 in this Teacher's Edition) for each student. You will distribute this page to students after the pretest.

During Say each word in boldface, read the context sentence, and then repeat the word. Have students write the words in the Pretest column on page 5 of the Student Book.

After Distribute to students a copy of the Answer Key/Shopping List page so that they can correct their pretests.

- Students should cross out any misspelled words and write the correct spelling. Words that were correctly spelled can be replaced with words from the Shopping List. Assign a list from which students should choose their words. (See below.)

- Be sure that each student has a list of eight correctly spelled words, which they should copy into the School and At-Home Lists and the Sorting Boxes (page 6).

Pretest context sentences (spelling word in bold):

1. Oh, look **at** the butterfly!
2. Last night we **ate** dinner at 6:00 o'clock.
3. Wear a **hat** so you don't get cold.
4. I **hate** broccoli, but I love spinach.
5. Make sure you put the **cap** back on the ketchup bottle.
6. The superhero wore a red **cape** and boots.
7. Just **tap** the button and the light will turn on.
8. Please hand me some **tape** so I can fix this torn page.

At-Home List
Send the At-Home List home so that families can help their students study the words and features. Several literacy activities are given on the back of the At-Home List. These include circling the spelling words embedded in a continuous chain of letters, creating rhymes with the spelling words, writing words with different colors for each vowel sound, and decoding words written in numerical code.

> **NOTE** The Shopping List provides words below grade level (column 1), words at grade level (column 2), and more challenging words that still have the feature (column 3).

Name _____

Answer Key

1. at
2. ate
3. hat
4. hate
5. cap
6. cape
7. tap
8. tape

Shopping List

bat   nap   brat
fat   pat   snap
late   grape   shape
gate   state   skate

Sorting Boxes

Day 2
Word Sorting

Explain to students that each week they will be looking carefully at their spelling words and deciding how to sort them into two or three groups. The words in each group will have something in common. The words might rhyme, or they might have the same letters or sounds at the beginning, in the middle, or at the end.

Have students cut out their Sorting Boxes to create word cards. They can then work in small groups or with partners to sort the words and come up with a way to describe what they have done. While students are learning to sort words at the beginning of the year, you might model the process before they attempt it on their own. You can use oversized word cards (CD-ROM) or a cut-up transparency (Transparency 2) and overhead to facilitate your model. Use the following Think Aloud with your visuals.

TEACHER'S THINK ALOUD All of my spelling cards have something in common. So, I am going to think and look and listen. [*Read each sorting card aloud.*] My eye sees that all my spelling cards have the vowel letter *a*. Some of them have the vowels *a* and *e*. My ear tells me that there are two different sounds of *a*. So I'm going to sort my spelling cards into two groups [*Begin to sort, using a pocket chart or some way so that cards are all visible and not on top of each other.*] In one column, the words have the short *a* sound: they all end in a consonant. The other words have the long *a* sound and end with an *e*, but I don't hear it. So, I predict that the silent *e* at the end of each of those words makes the *a* have a long vowel sound.

- After sorting, bring the class together to discuss the concept of a generalization. Explain, if necessary, that a generalization is a statement that describes a spelling pattern that works for many words. An example is this: *There are two sounds for the vowel* a. *The words that had the long sound of* a *all have a silent* e *at the end that I can see but can't hear.* Have students write their version on page 6 of the Student Book.

- You might also write the generalization on a sentence strip or poster to display for the duration of the lesson. Leave room for students to add some of their Prove It! words from Day 3.

- Students can preserve their word sorts by gluing the word cards to a separate sheet of paper. Otherwise, they can store their Sorting Boxes. (See page xi in this Teacher's Edition.)

Have students review the generalization and find more examples of words with long *a* and short *a* sounds in simple poetry and storybooks. Make sure students can read the words and that the words fit the generalization. You may want to adjust the number of words students should find, depending on students' needs. Have students share their lists with the class. Keep these lists in a class word bank or chart for future reference.

The goal of any spelling program is for students to be able to use their words in writing. Have students write simple sentences using their words. Encourage them to try to use more than one spelling word in each sentence. Remind them that the sentences do not have to be serious. They can be silly, as long as they make sense.

Remind students of the elements of a good sentence:

- A sentence tells a complete idea.

- A sentence has a subject, or naming part.

- A sentence has a verb, or telling part.

- The subject and verb must go together.

- Every sentence starts with a capital letter and ends with a punctuation mark.

Proofreading Tip Explain that proofreading and reading are different. When students read, their eyes sweep over the words to take in the meaning. They may not read every single word. However, when they proofread, they must be sure to look at the words slowly and carefully enough so that they can be sure all the words are correct. One way that they can check all the words is to read them out loud. This way, they can hear whether any words were left out or whether some words should be changed.

Word Stories Make sure that students know what a taco is: a sandwich-like food made from a soft or crisp corn tortilla folded over some type of filling. If students have eaten tacos, invite them to describe what they looked and tasted like. Then explain that the word *taco* comes from the Spanish language, which has contributed many words to English. In Spanish, the word *taco* means "snack." Have students tell why a taco would be a good snack. Ask what chili is (a spicy bean dish that sometimes contains meat). Explain that *chili* also comes from Spanish. It is the name of a spicy pepper that is used to flavor the food.

Day 5
Word Play and Posttest

Have students cut letter cards apart. See pages 189 and 190 in this Teacher's Edition) Show students how to take a letter, such as *b*, and put it next to -*ap* and -*at*. Ask which combination makes a word. Have students write *bat* in their books. Then have them work independently or in groups or teams to create other words. When students have finished, invite them to read their words aloud.

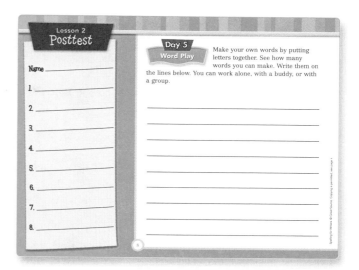

Posttest Have students tear out the perforated posttest. Students should pair up with their buddies or partners and exchange School Lists (page 5 in the Student Book). Students take turns testing each other on their respective spelling words. Collect the posttest sheets, score them, and record the correct response percentages (Teacher's Edition page 180). Mastery is 6 out of 8 words correct (75%). For students who do not achieve posttest mastery, see page xv in this Teacher's Edition.

Anchor Words After the posttest, have students select one or two anchor words to help them remember the word feature in this lesson. Record the words on the "Anchor Words" poster and refer to them in the Review lesson.

Lesson 3 — Short and Long e.

The short e sound can be spelled with e alone (*tell*). The long e sound can be spelled with *ea* or *ee* (*heat, peel*).

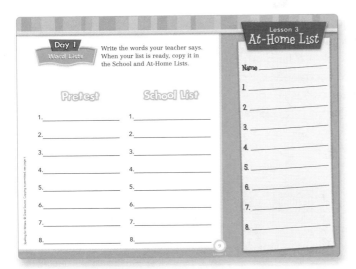

Day 1 — Pretest and Word Lists

Before Photocopy the Answer Key/ Shopping List page (page 11 in this Teacher's Edition) for each student.

During Say each word in boldface, read the context sentence, and then repeat the word. Have students write the words in the Pretest column on page 9 of the Student Book.

After Distribute to students a copy of the Answer Key/Shopping List page so that they can correct their pretests.

- Students should cross out any misspelled words and write the correct spelling. Words that were correctly spelled can be replaced with words from the Shopping List. Assign a list from which students should choose their words. (See below.)

- Be sure that each student has a list of eight correctly spelled words, which they should copy into the School and At-Home Lists and the Sorting Boxes (page 11).

Pretest context sentences (spelling word in bold):

1. Did you **eat** a good breakfast?
2. Please dry those **wet** dishes.
3. I like to **feel** wind against my face.
4. Rain **fell** from the sky.
5. This orange **peel** is hard to remove.
6. Can you **tell** me what time the store closes?
7. Your father has not **yet** returned from work.
8. The **heat** from the sun warms the rocks.

At-Home List Send the At-Home List home so that families can help their students study the words and features. Several literacy activities are given on the back of the At-Home List. They include illustrating the words, making crossword-puzzle pairs, using cut-out letters to spell words, and spelling words into someone else's hand.

> **NOTE** The Shopping List provides words below grade level (column 1), words at grade level (column 2), and more challenging words that still have the feature (column 3).

Name _____

Answer Key

1. eat	**5.** peel
2. wet	**6.** tell
3. feel	**7.** yet
4. fell	**8.** heat

Shopping List

bed	left	cent
net	each	ever
bee	free	peach
seed	sleep	asleep

Sorting Boxes

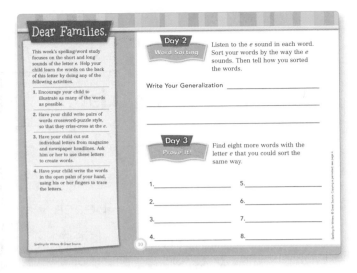

Have students cut out their Sorting Boxes to create word cards. They can then work in small groups or with partners to sort the words and come up with a generalization. Depending on how well your students understand the concept of sorting, you might decide to model the process either before or after they attempt it on their own. You can use oversized word cards (CD-ROM) or a cut-up transparency (Transparency 3) and overhead to facilitate your model. Use the following Think Aloud with your visuals.

TEACHER'S THINK ALOUD I know I need to use my brain, ears, and eyes when I read these cards. All of my spelling cards have something in common. So, I am going to think and look and listen. [*Read each sorting card aloud.*] My eye sees that all my spelling cards have the vowel letter *e*. Some of them have more than just the vowel letter *e*. My ear tells me that there are two different sounds of *e*. So I'm going to sort my spelling cards into two groups. [*Begin to sort, using a pocket chart or some way so that cards are all visible and not on top of each other.*] In one column, the words have the short *e* sound: they all have vowel letter *e* by itself. The other words have the long *e* sound and have another *e* or an *a* next to them, but I don't hear those vowels. So, I predict that the long *e* needs a second vowel beside it in order for it to make the long *e* sound.

- After students have sorted their words, bring the class together to reach a consensus about the generalization. An example is this: *The long vowel* e *had another vowel beside it that was silent. The short* e *vowel had a consonant next to it.* Have students write their version on Student book page 10 in the Student Book.

- Students can preserve their word sorts by gluing the word cards to a separate sheet of paper. Otherwise, they can store their Sorting Boxes. (See page xi in this Teacher's Edition.)

Day 3
Prove It!

Have students review the generalization and find more examples of words with short or long *e* sounds in leveled books, textbooks, and other sources. Make sure students can read the words and that the words fit the generalization. You may want to adjust the number of words students should find, depending on students' needs. Invite students to share their lists with partners or with the class. Keep these lists in a class word bank or chart for future reference.

Day 4
Spelling for Writing

The goal of any spelling program is for students to be able to use their words in writing. Have students write questions containing each word. Encourage them to try to use more than one word in each question.

Remind students of the elements of a good question:

- The subject and verb must go together.

- Every question starts with a capital letter.

- Every question ends with a question mark.

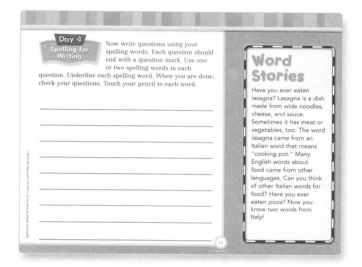

Proofreading Tip Remind students how reading and proofreading are different. Explain that the purpose of reading is to find out the meaning of a text, but the purpose of proofreading is to check the accuracy of a text. Demonstrate a method of checking each word by showing students how to touch every word with a finger or pencil point so that the eyes concentrate on one word at a time.

Word Stories Ask students if they have ever tasted lasagna or pizza. Discuss each food. Lasagna is a dish made with layers of pasta, sauce, and cheese, while pizza is a crust with a topping of sauce and cheese. Explain that both of these words come from the Italian language. In Italian, the word *lasagna* means "cooking pot." The original meaning of the word *pizza* is not entirely clear. Most people think it came from a word meaning "to bite." Have students discuss the connection between the old and new meanings of each word.

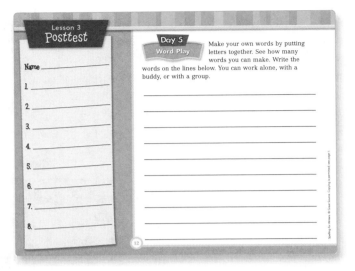

Have students cut letter cards apart. (See pages 189–190 in this Teacher's Edition.) Show students how to take a letter, such as *m,* and put it next to *-eat* and *-ell.* Ask which combination makes a word. Have students write *meat* in their books. Then have them work independently or in teams to create other words. When students have finished, invite them to read aloud their words, which you can add to the class word bank or chart.

Posttest Have students tear out the perforated posttest. Students should pair up with their buddies or partners and exchange School Lists (page 9 in the Student Book). Students take turns testing each other on their respective spelling words. Collect the posttest sheets, score them, and record the correct response percentages (Teacher's Edition page 180). Mastery is 6 out of 8 words correct (75%). For students who do not achieve posttest mastery, see page xv in this Teacher's Edition.

Anchor Words After the posttest, have students select one or two anchor words to help them remember the word feature in this lesson. Record the words on the "Anchor Words" poster and refer to them in the Review lesson.

Lesson 4

Short and Long _i._ A word spelled with a consonant-vowel-consonant (_CVC_) pattern usually has a short vowel sound (_fin_). A word spelled with a consonant-vowel-consonant-_e_ (_CVCe_) pattern usually has a long vowel sound (_fine_).

Day 1
Pretest and Word Lists

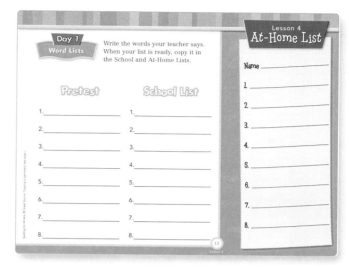

Before Photocopy the Answer Key/Shopping List page (page 16 in this Teacher's Edition) for each student.

During Say each word in boldface, read the context sentence, and then repeat the word. Have students write the words in the Pretest column on page 13 of the Student Book.

After Distribute to students a copy of the Answer Key/Shopping List page so that they can correct their pretests.

- Students should cross out any misspelled words and write the correct spelling. Words that were correctly spelled can be replaced with words from the Shopping List. Identify the list from which students should choose their words. (See below.)

- Be sure that each student has a list of eight correctly spelled words, which they should copy into the School and At-Home Lists and the Sorting Boxes (page 16).

Pretest context sentences (spelling word in bold):

1. The frightened dog **hid** under the bed.
2. I sat next to a new **kid** at school this week.
3. You go **hide**, and then I will try to find you.
4. My desk is on the left **side** of the room.
5. A needle has a hole in it, but a **pin** has no hole.
6. A **pine** tree has needles instead of leaves.
7. That shark has a big **fin** on its back.
8. I was sick yesterday, but I feel **fine** today.

At-Home List Send the At-Home List home so that families can help their students study the words and features. Several literacy activities are given on the back of the At-Home List. These include making word-search puzzles and spelling words using the numbers on a telephone keypad.

> **NOTE** The Shopping List provides words below grade level (column 1), words at grade level (column 2), and more challenging words that still have the feature (column 3).

Name _____

Shopping List

fit	fix	lift
lid	inch	quick
mice	price	pride
nice	prize	wider

Sorting Boxes

Day 2
Word Sorting

Have students cut out their Sorting Boxes to create word cards. They can then work in small groups or with partners to sort the words and come up with a generalization. Depending on how well your students understand the concept of sorting, you might decide to model the process either before or after they attempt it on their own. You can use oversized word cards (CD-ROM) or a cut-up transparency (Transparency 4) and overhead to facilitate your model. Use the following Think Aloud with your visuals.

Dear Families,

This week's spelling/word study focuses on the short and long sounds of the letter *i*. Help your child learn the words on the back of this letter by doing any of the following activities.

1. Help your child make a word-search puzzle using the week's words. Draw a grid, at least six squares across and six down. Have your child fill in the squares by writing spelling words across and down. Ask him or her to write one letter per square and to fill in the blank squares with random letters.

2. Help your child translate words into numbers using a telephone keypad. For example, the word *kid* would become 5-4-3. Have your child "spell" words using keypad numbers.

Spelling for Writers © Great Source

Day 2 Word Sorting Listen to the *i* sound in each word. Sort your words by the way the *i* sounds. Then write how you sorted the words.

Write Your Generalization _____

_____

_____

Day 3 Prove It! Find eight more words with the letter *i* that you could sort the same way.

1. _____   5. _____
2. _____   6. _____
3. _____   7. _____
4. _____   8. _____

TEACHER'S THINK ALOUD I know I need to use my brain, ears, and eyes when I read these cards. All of my spelling cards have something in common. So, I am going to think and look and listen. [*Read each sorting card aloud.*] My eye sees that all my spelling cards have the vowel letter *i*. Some of them have the vowels *i* and *e*. My ear tells me that there are two different sounds of *i*. So I'm going to sort my spelling cards into two groups. [*Begin to sort, using a pocket chart or some way so that cards are all visible and not on top of each other.*] In one column, the words have the short *i* sound: they all end in a consonant. The other words have the long *i* sound and end with an *e*, but I don't hear it. It must be silent. So, I predict that the silent *e* at the end of each of those words makes the *i* have a long vowel sound.

- After students have sorted their words, bring the class together to reach a consensus about the generalization. An example is this: *The words that have the long sound of* i *all have a silent* e *at the end that I can see, but I can't hear.* Have students write their version on page 14 of the Student Book.

- Remind students that they have seen the silent *e* marker before (Lesson 2) and that it sometimes works the same way with other vowels.

- You might also write the generalization on a sentence strip or poster to display for the duration of the lesson. Leave room for students to add some of their Prove It! words from Day 3.

- Students can preserve their word sorts by gluing the word cards to a separate sheet of paper. Otherwise, they can store their Sorting Boxes. (See page xi in this Teacher's Edition.)

Have students review the generalization and find more examples of words with a short or long *i* sound in simple poems, leveled books, and other sources. Make sure students can read the words and that the words fit the generalization. Adjust the materials students will use and the number of words they should find, according to their needs. Invite students to share their lists with partners or with the class. Keep these lists in a class word bank or chart for future reference.

Day 3
Prove It!

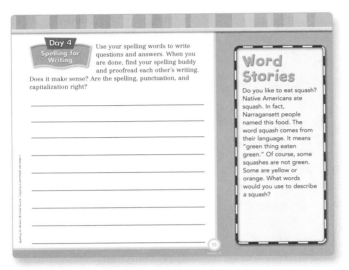

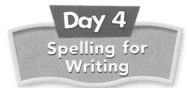

Day 4
Spelling for Writing

The goal of any spelling program is for students to be able to use their words in writing. Have students write questions and responses that contain their spelling words. Encourage them to try to use more than one spelling word in each: *for example, where did you hide the pin?*

Remind students of the elements of a good sentence:

- The subject and verb must go together.

- Every sentence starts with a capital letter and ends with a punctuation mark.

- Every question ends with a question mark.

Proofreading Tip Remind students how reading and proofreading are different. If you haven't already, demonstrate for the students how to touch every letter with a pencil to make sure that all the letters are correct and none were left out.

Word Stories Ask students if they have ever eaten squash, such as acorn squash or butternut squash. If not, describe it as a yellow vegetable that is often baked or mashed. Explain that the word *squash* came from a Native American language—specifically, from the Narragansett word *askutasquash*. When European settlers came to the New World, they found many foods that were new to them. Native Americans already had words for these foods. The words *pecan* (Illinois *pakani*) and *tomato* (Nahuatl *tomatl*) also came from Native American languages.

Day 5
Word Play and Posttest

Have students cut letter cards apart. (See pages 189–190 in this Teacher's Edition.) Show students how to take a letter, such as *l,* and put it next to *-id* and *-in.* Ask which combination makes a word. Have students write *lid* in their books. Then have them work independently or in teams to create other words. When students have finished, invite them to read their words aloud. You can add their words to the class word bank or chart.

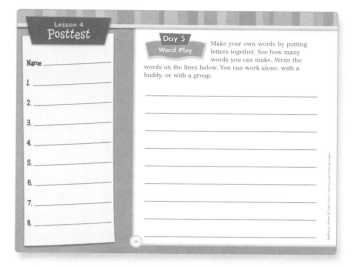

Posttest Have students tear out the perforated posttest. Students should pair up with their buddies or partners and exchange School Lists (page 13 in the Student Book). Students take turns testing each other on their respective spelling words. Collect the posttest sheets, score them, and record the correct response percentages (Teacher's Edition page 180). Mastery is 6 out of 8 words correct (75%). For students who do not achieve posttest mastery, see page xv in this Teacher's Edition.

Anchor Words After the posttest, have students select one or two anchor words to help them remember the word feature in this lesson. Record the words on the "Anchor Words" poster and refer to them in the Review lesson.

Periodically, check writing samples from your students for transfer of the word features that have been taught. The features for the last three lessons are as follows:

Lesson 2: Short and Long *a*
Lesson 3: Short and Long *e*
Lesson 4: Short and Long *i*

Lesson 5

Short and Long o. A word spelled with a consonant-vowel-consonant (*CVC*) pattern usually has a short vowel sound (*hop*). A word spelled with a consonant-vowel-consonant-*e* (*CVCe*) pattern usually has a long vowel sound (*hope*).

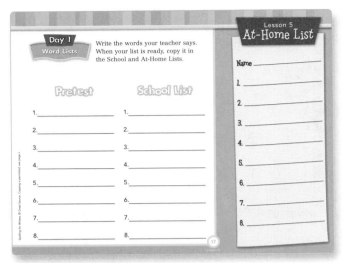

Day 1
Pretest and Word Lists

Before Photocopy the Answer Key/ Shopping List page (page 21 in this Teacher's Edition) for each student.

During Say each word in boldface, read the context sentence, and then repeat the word. Have students write the words in the Pretest column on page 17 of the Student Book.

After Distribute to students a copy of the Answer Key/Shopping List page so that they can correct their pretests.

- Students should cross out any misspelled words and write the correct spelling. Words that were correctly spelled can be replaced with words from the Shopping List. Assign a list from which students should choose their words. (See below.)

- Be sure that each student has a list of eight correctly spelled words, which they should copy into the School and At-Home Lists and the Sorting Boxes (page 21).

Pretest context sentences (spelling word in bold):

1. Do **not** cross the street.
2. Draw a **dot** in the middle of the circle.
3. I **hope** you like the present.
4. We can jump **rope** outside.
5. Now **hop** on one foot.
6. Put the book on the **top** shelf.
7. I dug a big **hole** in the sand.
8. The flag **pole** is very tall.

At-Home List Send the At-Home List home so that families can help their students study the words and features. Several literacy activities are given on the back of the At-Home List. These include making scrambled word puzzles, hiding words in a drawing, outlining words in several colors, and brainstorming rhyming words.

> **NOTE** The Shopping List provides words below grade level (column 1), words at grade level (column 2), and more challenging words that still have the feature (column 3).

Name

Answer Key

1. not   5. hop
2. dot   6. top
3. hope   7. hole
4. rope   8. pole

Shopping List

lot	crop	slot
pot	shot	dropped
those	joke	vote
bone	rode	drove

Sorting Boxes

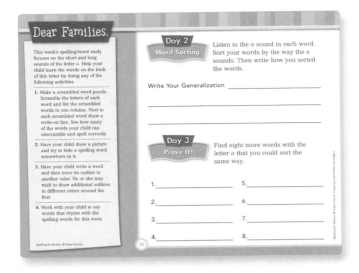

Have students cut out their Sorting Boxes to create word cards. They can then work in small groups or with partners to sort the words and come up with a generalization. You might decide to model the process either before or after they attempt it on their own. You can use oversized word cards (CD-ROM) or a cut-up transparency (Transparency 5) and overhead to facilitate your model.

Use the following Think Aloud with your visuals.

TEACHER'S THINK ALOUD I know I need to use my brain, ears, and eyes when I read these cards. All of my spelling cards have something in common. So, I am going to think and look and listen. [*Read each sorting card aloud.*] My eye sees that all my spelling cards have the vowel letter *o*. Some of them have the vowels *o* and *e*. My ear tells me that there are two different sounds of *o*. So I'm going to sort my spelling cards into two groups. [*Begin to sort, using a pocket chart or some way so that cards are all visible and not on top of each other.*] In one column, the words have the short *o* sound; they all end in a consonant. The other words have the long *o* sound and end with an *e*, but I don't hear it. It must be silent. So, I predict that the silent *e* at the end of each of those words makes the *o* have a long vowel sound.

- After students have sorted their words, bring the class together to reach a consensus about the generalization, such as this: *The words that have the long sound of* o *all have a silent* e *at the end that I can see, but I can't hear.* Have students write their version on page 18 of the Student Book.

- You might also write the generalization on a sentence strip or poster to display for the duration of the lesson. Leave room for students to add some of their Prove It! words from Day 3.

- Students can preserve their word sorts by gluing the word cards to a separate sheet of paper. Otherwise, they can store their Sorting Boxes. (See page xi in this Teacher's Edition.)

Day 3

Prove It!

Have students review the generalization and find more examples of words with a long or short *o* sound in picture books such as *Hop on Pop* (by Dr. Seuss), poems, and other reading materials such as magazines. Be sure students can read the words and that the words fit the generalization. Adjust the materials students will use and the number of words they should find, according to their needs. Invite students to share their lists with the class. Keep these lists in a class word bank or chart for future reference.

Day 4

Spelling for Writing

Give students an example of a sentence that might elicit "Oh, my!" For example, *I can hop for hours.* Then have students write sentences that might elicit "Oh, my!" as a response and that contain their spelling words. Encourage them to try to use more than one spelling word in each sentence.

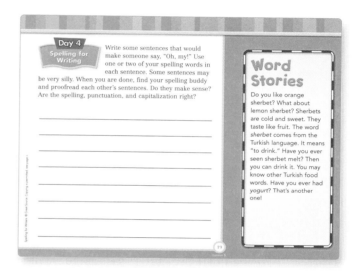

Remind students of the elements of any good sentence:

- The subject and verb must go together.

- Every sentence starts with a capital letter.

- Every sentence ends with a period, a question mark, or an exclamation point.

- The word *I* is always a capital letter.

Proofreading Tip Remind students that it is important for a proofreader to concentrate on only one word at a time. Placing a marker under a line of text helps the eyes to focus on individual words. Show students how to place a piece of paper under a line of text to do their proofreading.

Word Stories Ask students if they have ever tasted sherbet. If they have, ask them to describe it. If they have not, explain that sherbet is a little like ice cream. It is a cold, sweet dessert with a fruit flavor. Explain that the word *sherbet* comes from the Turkish language. It comes from a word meaning "to drink." Explain that sherbet starts as a fruit-flavored drink that is then frozen. Another word that comes from the Turkish language is *yogurt*. Yogurt, which is made from milk, is a popular food in Turkey.

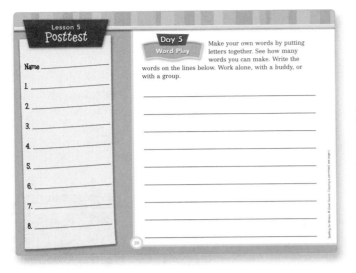

Have students cut letter cards apart. (See pages 189–190 in this Teacher's Edition.) Show students how to take a letter, such as *g,* and put it next to *-ot* and *-op.* Ask which combination makes a word. Have students write *got* in their books. Then have them work independently or in teams to create other words. When students have finished, invite them to read their words aloud. You can add their words to the class word bank or chart.

Posttest Have students tear out the perforated posttest. Students should pair up with their buddies or partners and exchange School Lists (page 17 in the Student Book). Students take turns testing each other on their respective spelling words. Collect the posttest sheets, score them, and record the correct response percentages (Teacher's Edition page 180). Mastery is 6 out of 8 words correct (75%). For students who do not achieve posttest mastery, see page xv in this Teacher's Edition.

Anchor Words After the posttest, have students select one or two anchor words to help them remember the word feature in this lesson. Record the words on the "Anchor Words" poster and refer to them in the Review lesson.

Lesson 6

Short and Long *u*. A word spelled with a consonant-vowel-consonant (*CVC*) pattern usually has a short vowel sound (*tub*). A word spelled with a consonant-vowel-consonant-e (*CVCe*) pattern usually has a long vowel sound (*tube*).

Day 1
Pretest and Word Lists

Before Photocopy the Answer Key/ Shopping List page (page 26 in this Teacher's Edition) for each student.

During Say each word in boldface, read the context sentence, and then repeat the word. Have students write the words on page 21 of the Student Book.

After Distribute to students a copy of the Answer Key/Shopping List page so that they can correct their pretests.

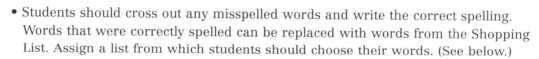

- Students should cross out any misspelled words and write the correct spelling. Words that were correctly spelled can be replaced with words from the Shopping List. Assign a list from which students should choose their words. (See below.)

- Be sure that each student has a list of eight correctly spelled words, which they should copy into the School and At-Home Lists and the Sorting Boxes (page 26).

Pretest context sentences (spelling word in bold):

1. What a **cute** little kitten!
2. I need a knife to **cut** this sandwich.
3. **Use** colored pencils to draw the flowers.
4. Our teacher showed **us** how to solve that problem.
5. Please empty the **tub** after your bath.
6. I can't get the cap off the **tube** of toothpaste.
7. A bear **cub** is just a baby bear.
8. A **cube** has a square on each side.

At-Home List Send the At-Home List home so that families can help their students study the words and features. Several literacy activities are given on the back of the At-Home List. These include making jigsaw puzzles with spelling words, making crossword pairs, writing the words and circling all the vowels, and arranging spelling words in alphabetical order.

NOTE The Shopping List provides words below grade level (column 1), words at grade level (column 2), and more challenging words that still have the feature (column 3).

Name _____

Answer Key

1. cute   5. tub
2. cut   6. tube
3. use   7. cub
4. us   8. cube

Shopping List

nut	but	shut
plus	just	grub
blue	June	true
glue	huge	due

Sorting Boxes

Day 2
Word Sorting

Have students cut out their Sorting Boxes to create word cards. They can then work in small groups or with partners to sort the words and come up with a generalization. You might decide to model the process either before or after they attempt it on their own. You can use oversized word cards (CD-ROM) or a cut-up transparency (Transparency 6) and overhead to facilitate your model. Use the following Think Aloud with your visuals.

Dear Families,

This week's spelling/word study focuses on the short and long sounds of the letter *u*. Help your child learn the words on the back of this letter by doing any of the following activities.

1. Have your child write the words in large letters on one sheet of paper. Then have him or her cut the paper into a jigsaw-type puzzle. Mix up the pieces and then solve the puzzle together.

2. Have your child write pairs of words crossword-puzzle style, crossing on the letter they share.

3. Have your child write the words and then circle all the vowels (*a, e, i, o, u*).

4. Help your child arrange the spelling words on the back of this letter in alphabetical order, the way they would appear in a dictionary.

Spelling for Writers © Great Source

Day 2 Word Sorting
Listen to the *u* sound in each word. Sort your words by the way the *u* sounds. Then write how you sorted the words.

Write Your Generalization _____

_____

_____

Day 3 Prove It!
Find eight more words with the letter *u* that you could sort the same way.

1._____ 5._____
2._____ 6._____
3._____ 7._____
4._____ 8._____

TEACHER'S THINK ALOUD I know I need to use my brain, ears, and eyes when I read these cards. All of my spelling cards have something in common. So, I am going to think and look and listen. [*Read each sorting card aloud.*] My eye sees that all my spelling cards have the vowel letter *u*. Some of them have the vowels *u* and *e*. My ear tells me that there are two different sounds of *u*. So I'm going to sort my spelling cards into two groups. [*Begin to sort, using a pocket chart or some way so that cards are all visible and not on top of each other.*] In one column, the words have the short *u* sound: they all end in a consonant. The other words have the long *u* sound and end with an *e*, but I don't hear it. It must be silent. So, I predict that the silent *e* at the end of each of those words makes the *u* have a long vowel sound.

- After students have sorted their words, bring the class together to reach a consensus about the generalization. An example is this: *The words that have the long sound of* u *all have a silent* e *at the end that I can see, but I can't hear.* Have students write their version on page 22 of the Student Book.

- You might also write the generalization on a sentence strip or poster to display for the duration of the lesson. Leave room for students to add some of their Prove It! words from Day 3.

- Students can preserve their sorts by gluing the word cards to a separate sheet of paper. Or, have students store their Sorting Boxes. (See page xi in this Teacher's Edition.)

Have students review the generalization and find more examples of words with a long or short *u* sound in leveled readers, poetry books, and magazines. Be sure students can read the words and that the words fit the generalization. Adjust the materials students will use and the number of words they should find, according to their needs. Invite students to share their lists with the class. Keep these lists in a class word bank or chart for future reference.

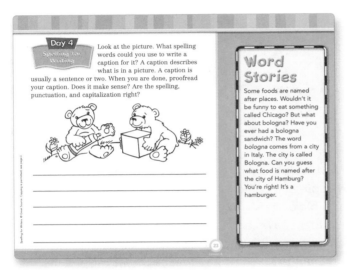

Show students an example of a picture caption. Briefly discuss what a caption does and its connection to the image. Then have students write captions using their spelling words. Encourage them to write in complete sentences.

Remind students of the elements of any good sentence:

- The subject and verb must go together.

- Every sentence starts with a capital letter.

- Every sentence ends with a period, a question mark, or an exclamation point.

Proofreading Tip Teach students to look *for* something. Explain that they should check for one thing at a time, for example, mistakes that each student knows he or she makes consistently, punctuation at the end of each sentence, capital letters at the beginning of each sentence, or spelling.

Word Stories Ask students if they have ever tasted bologna. If they have, ask them to describe what it looks and tastes like. If they have not, explain that bologna is a type of large sausage made from meat. It is sliced and then heated or served cold in sandwiches. Explain that the word *bologna* comes from the name of a place—the city of Bologna, Italy. It is not the only food word that is named for a place. Hamburgers are named for Hamburg, Germany. Have students tell what they like to eat with hamburgers.

Day 5
Word Play and Posttest

Have students cut letter cards apart. (See pages 189–190 in this Teacher's Edition.) Show students how to take letters, such as *s* and *h,* and put them next to *-ut* and *-ub.* Ask which combination makes a word. Have students write *shut* in their books. Then have them work independently or in teams to create other words. When students have finished, invite them to read their words aloud.

Posttest Have students tear out the perforated posttest. Students should pair up with their buddies or partners and exchange School Lists (page 21 in the Student Book). Students take turns testing each other on their respective spelling words. Collect the posttest sheets, score them, and record the correct response percentages (Teacher's Edition page 180). Mastery is 6 out of 8 words correct (75%). For students who do not achieve posttest mastery, see page xv in this Teacher's Edition.

Anchor Words After the posttest, have students select one or two anchor words to help them remember the word feature in this lesson. Record the words on the "Anchor Words" poster and refer to them in the Review lesson.

Lesson 7 — Long Vowels (final *y*).

When a word ends with a long vowel sound, the sound is probably spelled with *y* or a vowel plus *y* (*many, my, play.*)

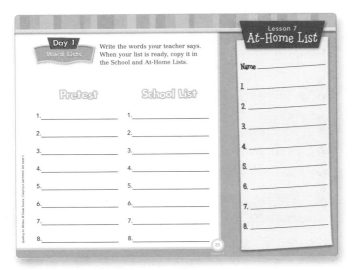

Day 1
Pretest and Word Lists

Before Photocopy the Answer Key/ Shopping List page (page 31 in this Teacher's Edition) for each student.

During Say each word in boldface, read the context sentence, and then repeat the word. Have students write the words in the Pretest column on page 25 of the Student Book.

After Distribute to students a copy of the Answer Key/Shopping List page so that they can correct their pretests.

- Students should cross out any misspelled words and write the correct spelling. Words that were correctly spelled can be replaced with words from the Shopping List. Assign a list from which students should choose their words. (See below.)

- Be sure that each student has a list of eight correctly spelled words, which they should copy into the School and At-Home Lists and the Sorting Boxes (page 31).

Pretest context sentences (spelling word in bold):

1. This flower opens during the **day** and closes at night.
2. Those yellow flowers look **pretty** in that blue bowl.
3. Your parents said that **they** will pick you up after school.
4. I brush **my** teeth every day.
5. I like to **play** with blocks.
6. Yesterday was warm, so **many** people wore shorts.
7. **Why** are you so happy today?
8. Our new puppy is **very** small, but it will grow.

At-Home List Send the At-Home List home so that families can help their students study the words and features. Several literacy activities are given on the back of the At-Home List: drawing words using different colors for different vowel sounds, having a "Word Hunt" using old magazines, and playing "Backwards Hink Pink."

> **NOTE** The Shopping List provides words below grade level (column 1), words at grade level (column 2), and more challenging words (column 3).

Name _____

Shopping List

say	pray	spray
stay	clay	hay
fly	eye	goodbye
key	worry	sleepy

Sorting Boxes

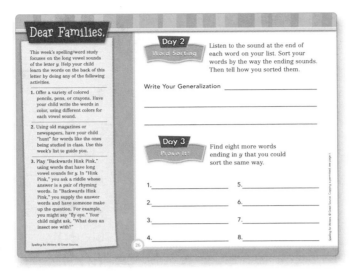

Day 2
Word Sorting

Have students cut out their Sorting Boxes to create word cards. They can then work in small groups or with partners to sort the words and come up with a generalization. You might decide to model the process either before or after they attempt it on their own. You can use oversized word cards (CD-ROM) or a cut-up transparency (Transparency 7) and overhead to facilitate your model.

Use the following Think Aloud with your visuals.

TEACHER'S THINK ALOUD I am going to use my eyes and ears to see what my words have in common. [*Read each sorting card aloud.*] My eye sees that all my spelling cards have the vowel letter *y*. My ear tells me that the words ends with three different long vowel sounds. So I'm going to sort my spelling cards into three groups [*Begin to sort, using a pocket chart or some way so that cards are all visible and not on top of each other.*] In one column, the words have the long *i* sound; they all end in a vowel *y*. In the second column, the words have the long *e* sound; they also end in vowel *y*. The words in the third column have the long *a* sound but end in *ay*. So, I predict that when a word ends with a long vowel sound, the sound is spelled with *y* or *ay*.

- Have students sort the words from their own lists. Circulate around the classroom and have each group or pair describe their method of sorting.

- Bring the class together to reach a consensus about the generalization, such as this: *The long* e *or* i *sound at the end of a word can be spelled with* y. *The long* a *sound at the end of a word can be spelled with* ay. Have students write their version on page 26 of the Student Book.

- You might also write the generalization on a sentence strip or poster to display for the duration of the lesson. Leave room for students to add some of their Prove It! words from Day 3.

- Students can preserve their word sorts by gluing the word cards to a separate sheet of paper. Otherwise, they can store their Sorting Boxes. (See page xi in this Teacher's Edition.)

Day 3
Prove It!

Have students review the generalization and find more examples in available materials, such as stories, poems, magazines, or textbooks. Be sure that students can read the words and that the words prove the generalization. Adjust the materials students will use and the number of words they should find, according to their needs. Invite students to share their lists with the class. Keep these lists in a class word bank or chart for future reference.

Day 4
Spelling for Writing

Draw a sample Word Wheel on the board, using the one on Student Book page 27 as a model. Write a spelling word in the center. Then have the students help you think of rhyming words to write around the outer part of the circle. Note that some of the rhyming words will have the same spelling pattern as the spelling word; some will not. Students will make a Word Wheel in the Student Book, but encourage them to make more wheels on their own paper.

> **Day 4**
> **Spelling for Writing**
> Choose a spelling word to make a rhyming word wheel. Write the word in the middle. Write rhyming words all around it. Make wheels for your other words on your own paper. When you are finished, make sure the words are spelled correctly.
>
> **Word Stories**
> Have you ever eaten tofu? Tofu is a soft, white food. Many people eat tofu in place of meat. The word tofu comes from the Japanese language. It means "bean curd." Tofu is made from soybean curds. First the soybeans are cooked. This makes a kind of milk. Parts of the milk form clumps. These are the curds. Tofu is made from the curds.

Remind students of the elements of a good Word Wheel:

- Every word in the wheel should end with the same sound.

- The sound may be spelled in different ways.

Proofreading Tip Instruct the students to read the words aloud to make sure that no words were left out.

Word Stories Ask students if they have ever eaten tofu. If they have, ask them to describe what it looks and feels like. If not, explain that tofu is a food that looks and feels like a soft, white cheese. Unlike cheese, which is made from animals' milk, tofu is made from soybean curd. Explain that the word *tofu* comes from the Japanese language. If necessary, have students find Japan on a map. Point out that tofu is used in many foods from Japan, China, Korea, and other countries in southeast Asia. Tofu has been around for many centuries. It may first have appeared in China during the Han Dynasty (206 B.C. to A.D. 220).

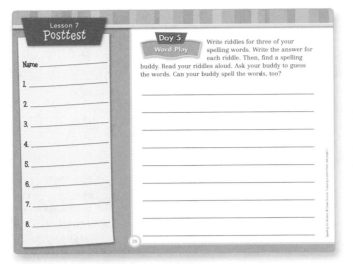

Students will choose three of their spelling words and write a riddle, with its answer, for each word. Then, students will ask a partner the riddles. The partner is to guess the word and spell it, too. This is a way for students to generalize the word features they have learned because some students will have different words from their partners.

Posttest Have students tear out the perforated posttest. Students should pair up with their buddies or partners and exchange School Lists (page 25 in the Student Book). Students take turns testing each other on their respective spelling words. Collect the posttest sheets, score them, and record the correct response percentages (Teacher's Edition page 180). Mastery is 6 out of 8 words correct (75%). For students who do not achieve posttest mastery, see page xv in this Teacher's Edition.

Anchor Words After the posttest, have students select one or two anchor words to help them remember the word feature in this lesson. Record the words on the "Anchor Words" poster and refer to them in the Review lesson.

Periodically, check writing samples from your students for transfer of the word features that have been taught. The features for the last three lessons are as follows:

Lesson 5: Short and Long *o*
Lesson 6: Short and Long *u*
Lesson 7: Long Vowels *(final y)*

Lesson 8 Review (Lessons 2–7).

Day 1
Pretest and Word Lists

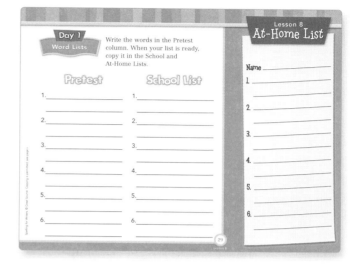

Before There are three options for selecting the pretest words. Choose the one most appropriate for your students.

1. Have students think of words that fit the spelling patterns and write them.

2. Use the words that you and your class collected on the "Anchor Words" poster.

3. Use the examples given on page 36.

If you will dictate the words, either from the "Anchor Words" poster or from page 36, make an answer key by writing the words on a copy of Copy Master 1. Photocopy the filled-in answer key page for each student.

During Announce each word feature as listed on page 36. As you say each feature, also state the generalization and give the words or ask students to think of words. Students will write two words for each feature on page 29 of the Student Book.

After If you dictated words, distribute a copy of the answer key so that students can self-correct their pretests. Otherwise, correct students' pretests.

• For any word that students got correct, send them back to the lesson for that feature to select a word from their Prove It! List they want to learn to spell.

• Be sure that each student has a list of correctly spelled words, which they should copy into the School and At-Home Lists and the Sorting Boxes (use Copy Master 1 for the Sorting Boxes).

At-Home List Send the At-Home List home so that families can use the following activities with their children: "show and tell" vowel sounds, salt or sand spelling, and rhyming words.

Word Features and Generalizations

1. **Short and Long *a*.** A word spelled with a consonant-vowel-consonant (CVC) pattern usually has a short vowel sound (*cap*). A word spelled with a consonant-vowel-consonant-*e* (CVCe) pattern usually has a long vowel sound (*cape*). (*Lesson 2*)

2. **Short and Long *e*.** The short *e* sound can be spelled with *e* alone (*tell*). The long *e* sound can be spelled with *ea* or *ee* (*heat*). (*Lesson 3*)

3. **Short and Long *i*.** A word spelled with a consonant-vowel-consonant (CVC) pattern usually has a short vowel sound (*fin*). A word spelled with a consonant-vowel-consonant-*e* (CVCe) pattern usually has a long vowel sound (*fine*). (*Lesson 4*)

4. **Short and Long *o*.** A word spelled with a consonant-vowel-consonant (CVC) pattern usually has a short vowel sound (*hop*). A word spelled with a consonant-vowel-consonant-*e* (CVCe) pattern usually has a long vowel sound (*hope*). (*Lesson 5*)

5. **Short and Long *u*.** A word spelled with a consonant-vowel-consonant (CVC) pattern usually has a short vowel sound (*tub*). A word spelled with a consonant-vowel-consonant-*e* (CVCe) pattern usually has a long vowel sound (*tube*). (*Lesson 6*)

6. **Long Vowels (final *y*).** When a word ends with the sound of long *a, e,* or *i,* it probably ends with the letter *y* (*my*) or a vowel plus *y* (*play*). (*Lesson 7*)

Day 2
Word Sorting

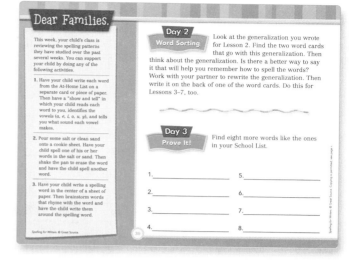

Students will revisit the generalizations they wrote for Lessons 2–7. The goal is to be sure students understand them and also to rewrite them more clearly, if necessary.

- Have students cut apart the Sorting Boxes to create word cards for this activity (Copy Master 1).

- Have students form pairs and turn to page 6 of the Student Book.

- Both students should read the generalization they wrote for Lesson 2 and identify the two word cards that relate to this generalization. Then they should think about how the generalization is written. Is the meaning clear? Is there a way to state the generalization that is more helpful in remembering how to spell the words?

- You might work through the first generalization as a class to show students how to clarify and improve the wording.

- Students should then write the revised generalization on the back of a relevant word card and move on to the next generalization (Lesson 3).

As a closing step, have students work in pairs to sort their words into groups that make sense. Circulate through the room to talk with students about their word sorts. Students' explanations of their sorts tell you what they understand about how words work.

After students revisit and revise several generalizations for this lesson's review, send them off to find in readable materials more examples that prove as many of the generalizations as possible to be true. Provide appropriate reading materials, such as storybooks, poetry books, newspapers, and textbooks. Be sure that students can read the words they find and that their words prove each generalization. You might want to limit the scope of the word hunt by having some students search for words that prove only one or two of the generalizations. Invite students to share their lists with the class. Keep these lists in a class word bank or chart for future reference.

Day 3

Prove It!

Day 4

Spelling for Writing

Day 4
Spelling for Writing

Write a story that uses some of your spelling words. First look at all your words. Which ones give you ideas for a story? Then write your story on the lines below. Underline all the spelling words. Check each word to be sure it is spelled correctly.

Word Stories

Have you ever had an omelet for breakfast? A plain omelet is very simple. It is just eggs that are beaten, poured into a pan, cooked flat, and then folded over. The word *omelet* comes from an old French word that means "a thin plate" or "the blade of a knife." An omelet is thin until you add fillings. With cheese, vegetables, and meat inside, an omelet can become quite fat!

Students should work individually to write their stories, although they might work with partners to brainstorm ideas before they write. Encourage them to use as many spelling words as possible in their stories, including words from the word hunt. The words themselves should suggest ideas for stories and characters—for example, the word *cape* could be part of a superhero's costume.

Offer these tips for writing stories:

• Write about just one event.

• Use words that help the reader see the action and where the story takes place.

• Use some dialogue for the characters.

Proofreading Tip Remind students that reading and proofreading are different. Suggest that students read their writing aloud so that they can hear how the words fit together. Sometimes reading aloud helps point out where words are missing or where a better word might be used. Reading out loud also helps slow down the eyes so that they can focus on each word.

Word Stories Ask if any students have ever watched someone make an omelet. If so, have a volunteer describe what the beaten eggs look like when they are poured into the pan. (They form a thin, flat circle.) Ask how this relates to the meaning of the old French word *alumelle*, which means "thin plate" or "the blade of a sword or knife." This word evolved into the modern French word *omelette*. The omelet was named for its flat, thin shape.

Day 5
Word Play and Posttest

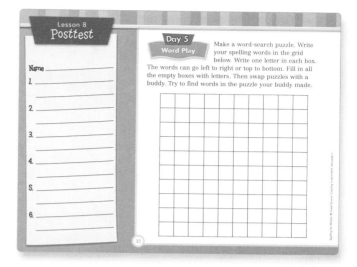

If possible, show students a word-find puzzle in a book of puzzles or on the overhead projector. Show how the words can be spelled across, down, or diagonally. Review the directions on page 32 of the Student Book and make sure students understand how to use the grid to make their own puzzles. When students have completed their puzzles, have them swap with partners and hunt for the hidden words. Suggest that students write out an answer key on a separate sheet of paper. This will help the word finder know what to look for.

Review Activities Other activities that students can do to review the words include the following:

- Have students choose a set of Sorting Boxes from a previous lesson and time themselves when they sort the cards. Students should sort them several times to see whether their sorting time gets faster. (Copy Masters of the pretest words can be found in the Transparencies and Copy Masters folder. Or, generate word cards from the CD-ROM.)

- Students can use their review list in a Word Play activity from a previous lesson or to make another word-find puzzle, as in this lesson.

- Generate a practice activity from the CD-ROM.

Posttest Have students carefully tear out the posttest form on Student Book page 32. Students should pair up with their buddies or partners and exchange School Lists (page 29 in the Student Book). Students take turns testing each other on their respective spelling words. Collect the posttest sheets and score them. Mastery is 10 out of 12, or 80%. For students who do not achieve posttest mastery, see page xv in this Teacher's Edition.

Lesson 9 Short Vowels (*a, i*). A word spelled with a consonant-vowel-consonant (*CVC*) pattern usually has a short sound (*bag, six*).

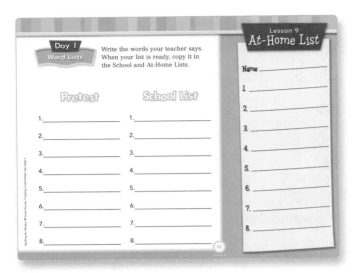

Day 1 Pretest and Word Lists

Before Photocopy the Answer Key/Shopping List page (page 41 in this Teacher's Edition) for each student.

During Say each word in boldface, read the context sentence, and then repeat the word. Have students write the words in the Pretest column on page 33 of the Student Book.

After Distribute to students a copy of the Answer Key/Shopping List page so that they can correct their pretests.

- Students should cross out any misspelled words and write the correct spelling. Words that were correctly spelled can be replaced with words from the Shopping List. Assign a list from which students should choose their words. (See below.)

- Be sure that each student has a list of eight correctly spelled words, which they should copy into the School and At-Home Lists and the Sorting Boxes (page 41).

Pretest context sentences (spelling word in bold):

1. My lunch is in a brown paper **bag**.
2. Be as quiet **as** a mouse!
3. Try to **hit** the ball with the bat.
4. I'll wear a red shirt with my **tan** pants.
5. You may invite **six** friends to your party.
6. I **sat** down in my seat.
7. **Dig** a deep hole for that plant.
8. I want to **win** that contest.

At-Home List Send the At-Home List home so that families can help their students study the words and features. Several literacy activities are given on the back of the At-Home List: hunting for words in print sources, creating rhyming lists, and illustrating words.

> **NOTE** The Shopping List provides words below grade level (column 1), words at grade level (column 2), and more challenging words that still have the feature (column 3).

Name _____

Answer Key

1. bag	**5.** six
2. as	**6.** sat
3. hit	**7.** dig
4. tan	**8.** win

Shopping List

can	lad	began
has	math	mask
pin	list	middle
trip	into	gift

Sorting Boxes

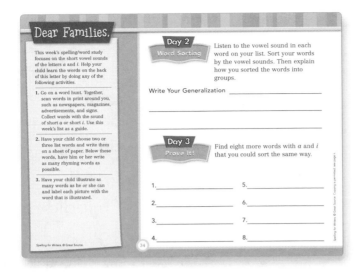

Have students cut out their Sorting Boxes to create word cards. They can then work in small groups or with partners to sort the words and come up with a generalization. You might decide to model the process either before or after they attempt it on their own. You can use oversized word cards (CD-ROM) or a cut-up transparency (Transparency 8) and overhead to facilitate your model.

Use the following Think Aloud with your visuals.

> **TEACHER'S THINK ALOUD** I am going to think and look and listen to all my words. [*Read each word card aloud.*] My eye sees that all my spelling cards have at least one vowel letter. Some of them have the vowel letter *a* and some have the vowel letter *i*. When I say *bag* and *hit*, I think to myself that these words have a short vowel sound. I will sort my words by the vowel sound.

- Have students sort the words from their own lists. Circulate around the classroom and have each group or pair describe their method of sorting.

- Bring the class together to reach a consensus about the generalization. An example is this: *When I sorted my words I discovered two different vowel sounds, short* a *as in* bag *and short* i *as in* hit. Have students write their version on page 34 of the Student Book.

- Point out that the sound of a short vowel is often spelled with one vowel next to (before) a consonant.

- You might also write the generalization on a sentence strip or poster to display for the duration of the lesson. Leave room for students to add some of their Prove It! words from Day 3.

- Students can preserve their word sorts by gluing the word cards to a separate sheet of paper. Otherwise, they can store their Sorting Boxes. (See page xi in this Teacher's Edition.)

Day 3
Prove It!

Have students review the generalization of words with a short *a* or short *i* sound and find more examples in available materials, such as simple storybooks, poetry books, or textbooks. Be sure that students can read the words and that the words prove the generalization. You may want to adjust the number of words students should find, depending on students' needs. Invite students to share their lists with the class. Keep these lists in a class word bank or chart for future reference.

Day 4
Spelling for Writing

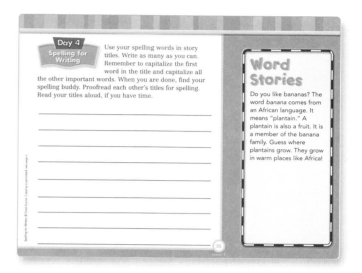

Write the word *trip* on the board. Suggest one or two titles that could be made using that word, such as "My Best (or Worst) Trip" or "A Trip to the Moon." Write these on the board. Then ask volunteers to suggest other titles. Students should then work independently to create their own story titles.

Remind students of the elements of a good title:

- The first word should always be capitalized.

- Every important word in the title should be capitalized.

- A little word, such as *the*, is not capitalized unless it is the first word.

Proofreading Tip Remind students that proofreading must be done slowly and carefully. On a large piece of text, demonstrate how to touch every word with a finger or pencil so that the eyes concentrate on one word at a time.

Word Stories Ask students to describe a banana. Have them raise their hands if they like to eat bananas. Explain that the word *banana* comes from an African language (more specifically, from the Wolof, Mandingo, and Fulani languages of West Africa). It comes from a word that means "plantain." A plantain is a kind of banana. Plantains and bananas both grow in warm places, like Africa. However, people cook plantains before eating them, while bananas are usually not cooked. Another food word from this language is *yam*. Ask students if they have ever tasted yams, which are like sweet potatoes. If they have not, explain that yams are yellow and have a sweet taste. The word *yam* comes from another West African word that means "to eat."

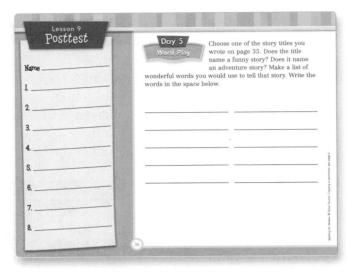

Have students select one title that they created during Spelling for Writing. Tell them to select the title that they think would make the most interesting story. Encourage them to name characters, places, or events that might be in that story. Then have them work independently or in groups to list wonderful words for their stories. When students have finished, invite them to read their words aloud, which you can add to the class word bank or chart.

Posttest Have students tear out the perforated posttest. Students should pair up with their buddies or partners and exchange School Lists (page 33 in the Student Book). Students take turns testing each other on their respective spelling words. Collect the posttest sheets, score them, and record the correct response percentages (Teacher's Edition page 180). Mastery is 6 out of 8 words correct (75%). For students who do not achieve posttest mastery, see page xv in this Teacher's Edition.

Anchor Words After the posttest, have students select one or two anchor words to help them remember the word feature in this lesson. Record the words on the "Anchor Words" poster and refer to them in the Review lesson.

Lesson 10

Short Vowels (e, o). A word spelled with a consonant-vowel-consonant (CVC) pattern usually has a short sound (*fox, ten*).

Day 1
Pretest and Word Lists

Before Photocopy the Answer Key/Shopping List page (page 46 in this Teacher's Edition) for each student.

During Say each word in boldface, read the context sentence, and then repeat the word. Have students write the words in the Pretest column on page 37 of the Student Book.

After Distribute to students a copy of the Answer Key/Shopping List page so that they can correct their pretests.

- Students should cross out any misspelled words and write the correct spelling. Words that were correctly spelled can be replaced with words from the Shopping List. Assign a list from which students should choose their words. (See below.)

- Be sure that each student has a list of eight correctly spelled words, which they should copy into the School and At-Home Lists and the Sorting Boxes (page 46).

Pretest context sentences (spelling word in bold):

1. I **went** right home after school.
2. Is that animal a **fox** or a wolf?
3. You have an ink **spot** on your hand.
4. Please **set** the glasses on the table.
5. You will need a broom and a **mop**.
6. **Nod** your head if you agree.
7. Will you **help** me solve this puzzle?
8. A dime is worth **ten** pennies.

At-Home List Send the At-Home List home so that families can help their students study the words and features. Several literacy activities are given on the back of the At-Home List: writing words crossword-puzzle style, circling words in a word chain, writing words with different colors for vowels and consonants, and creating a poem with rhyming words.

NOTE The Shopping List provides words below grade level (column 1), words at grade level (column 2), and more challenging words that still have the feature (column 3).

Day 1
Word Lists

Write the words your teacher says. When your list is ready, copy it in the School and At-Home Lists.

Pretest

1. _____
2. _____
3. _____
4. _____
5. _____
6. _____
7. _____
8. _____

School List

1. _____
2. _____
3. _____
4. _____
5. _____
6. _____
7. _____
8. _____

Lesson 10
At-Home List

Name _____

1. _____
2. _____
3. _____
4. _____
5. _____
6. _____
7. _____
8. _____

Name _____

Answer Key

1. went	**5.** mop
2. fox	**6.** nod
3. spot	**7.** help
4. set	**8.** ten

Shopping List

red	less	when
yes	spell	then
on	long	body
got	gone	odd

Sorting Boxes

Day 2
Word Sorting

Have students cut out their Sorting Boxes to create word cards. They can then work in small groups or with partners to sort the words and come up with a way to describe how they chose the groups. You might decide to model the process either before or after they attempt it on their own. You can use oversized word cards (CD-ROM) or a cut-up transparency (Transparency 9) and overhead to facilitate your model. Use the following Think Aloud with your visuals.

TEACHER'S THINK ALOUD I am going to look at my words. My eye sees that all my spelling cards have at least one vowel letter. Some of them have the vowel letter *e* and some have the vowel letter *o*. Now I'm going to listen as I say these words and think about what I hear. [*Compare and contrast words, such* ten *and* mop.] When I compare these words I think to myself, all of my words have a short vowel sound, and some of them have the short vowel sound of *e* as in *ten,* and some of them have the short vowel sound of *o* as in *mop.*

- Have students sort the words from their own lists. Circulate around the classroom and have each group or pair describe their method of sorting.

- Bring the class together to reach a consensus about the generalization, such as this: *When I sorted my words I discovered two different vowel sounds, short* e *as in* ten *and short* o *as in* mop. Have students write their version on page 38 of their Student Book.

- Remind students that a short vowel sound is often spelled with one vowel followed by one or two consonants.

- You might also write the generalization on a sentence strip or poster to display for the duration of the lesson. Leave room for students to add some of their Prove It! words from Day 3.

- Students can preserve their word sorts by gluing the word cards to a separate sheet of paper. Otherwise, they can store their Sorting Boxes. (See page xi in this Teacher's Edition.)

Have students review the generalization and find more examples in available materials, such as simple storybooks, rhyming books, or labeled picture books. Be sure that students can read the words and that the words prove the generalization. You may want to adjust the number of words students should find, depending on students' needs. Invite students to share their lists with the class. Keep these lists in a class word bank or chart for future reference.

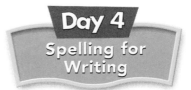

Students will write a narrative about a time they helped someone do something. Before students start writing, spend some time talking about ideas that they can use in their writing. Make a list so that students will have ideas to choose from. Tell students to use as many spelling words and Prove It! words as they can.

Offer these tips to students:

- Describe just one event.

- Tell about the event in the order things happened.

- Use details that will help the reader make pictures in his or her mind.

Proofreading Tip Demonstrate for the students how to touch every letter with a pencil to make sure that all the letters are correct and none were left out.

Word Stories Ask students if they have ever sat outside on a patio. If so, have them describe it. If not, explain that a patio is a bit like an outdoor room. It has a floor but no ceiling. Some patios have walls around them, while others are open. If possible, show students pictures of patios, courtyards, decks, and porches (perhaps from a home improvement book or magazine). Discuss why people might enjoy having a patio and what they might do on one (sit outside in warm weather, have a meal,). Point out that while sitting outside in the summer, people might see some mosquitoes. The word *mosquito*, meaning "little fly," is also from the Spanish language.

Day 5
Word Play and Posttest

Show students a dictionary. Ask how they can find words in a dictionary. Discuss alphabetical order and places where it is used (telephone directory, class lists). If necessary, write the alphabet on the board and have students locate the initial letters of their names. Remind them that when two names begin with the same letter or letters, the names are alphabetized using the next letter. Demonstrate this, using two students' names (for example, John, Juan). Then have students complete the page. When they have finished, invite them to check their lists and read them aloud.

Lesson 10
Posttest

Name _____

1. _____
2. _____
3. _____
4. _____
5. _____
6. _____
7. _____
8. _____

Day 5
Word Play

List your words in alphabetical order. This is the order in which they appear in a dictionary. Words that begin with *a* come before words that begin with *b*. If two words begin with the same letter, look at the next letter. For example, *sat* would come before *sit*, because *a* comes before *i* in the alphabet.

1. _____
2. _____
3. _____
4. _____
5. _____
6. _____
7. _____
8. _____

Posttest Have students tear out the perforated posttest. Students should pair up with their buddies or partners and exchange School Lists (page 37 in the Student Book). Students take turns testing each other on their respective spelling words. Collect the posttest sheets, score them, and record the correct response percentages (Teacher's Edition page 180). Mastery is 6 out of 8 words correct (75%). For students who do not achieve posttest mastery, see page xv in this Teacher's Edition.

Anchor Words After the posttest, have students select one or two anchor words to help them remember the word feature in this lesson. Record the words on the "Anchor Words" poster and refer to them in the Review lesson.

Lesson 11

Short and Long Vowels (u, y). The short *u* is spelled with *u* (*sun*). A long vowel sound at the end of a word is often spelled with y or a vowel plus y (*sky, say*).

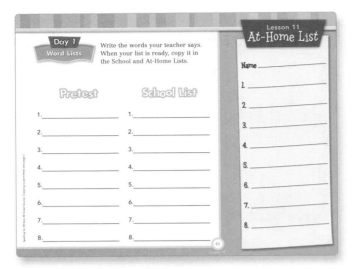

Before Photocopy the Answer Key/ Shopping List page (page 51 in this Teacher's Edition) for each student.

During Say each word in boldface, read the context sentence, and then repeat the word. Have students write the words in the Pretest column on page 41 of the Student Book.

After Distribute to students a copy of the Answer Key/Shopping List page so that they can correct their pretests.

- Students should cross out any misspelled words and write the correct spelling. Words that were correctly spelled can be replaced with words from the Shopping List. Assign a list from which students should choose their words. (See below.)

- Be sure that each student has a list of eight correctly spelled words, which they should copy into the School and At-Home Lists and the Sorting Boxes (page 51).

Pretest context sentences (spelling word in bold):

1. You have **mud** on your shoes.
2. I don't see a cloud in the **sky** today.
3. Do you walk to school or ride on a **bus**?
4. Remember to **say** "thank you."
5. A **bug** landed on the arm of my wheelchair and then flew away.
6. I know another **way** to make paper airplanes.
7. I did not hit the ball this time, but I will **try** again.
8. The **sun** is shining today.

At-Home List Send the At-Home List home so that families can help their students study the words and features. Several literacy activities are given on the back of the At-Home List: illustrating words, using the initial letters of words to write other words, and substituting vowels.

> **NOTE** The Shopping List provides words below grade level (column 1), words at grade level (column 2), and more challenging words that still have the feature. (column 3).

Name _____

Shopping List

jug   drug   stuff
duck   under   shrub
shy   penny   money
fly   myself   sway

Sorting Boxes

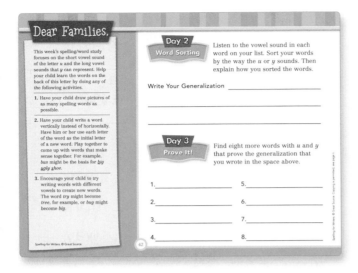

Day 2
Word Sorting

Listen to the vowel sound in each word on your list. Sort your words by the way the *u* or *y* sounds. Then explain how you sorted the words.

Write Your Generalization _____

_____

_____

Day 3
Prove It!

Find eight more words with *u* and *y* that prove the generalization that you wrote in the space above.

1._____   5._____

2._____   6._____

3._____   7._____

4._____   8._____

42

Day 2
Word Sorting

Have students cut out their Sorting Boxes to create word cards. They can then work in small groups or with partners to sort the words and come up with a way to describe how they chose the groups. You might decide to model the process either before or after they attempt it on their own. You can use oversized word cards (CD-ROM) or a cut-up transparency (Transparency 10) and overhead to facilitate your model. Use the following Think Aloud with your visuals.

TEACHER'S THINK ALOUD When I look at my words, I see that they have at least one vowel letter because I know that *y* can be a vowel. When I compare these words, I hear the short vowel sound for *u* (*sun*) and a long vowel sound for *y* (*sky*). So, I can sort my words into two groups, the short *u* sound and the long vowel sounds of *y*. All of my short *u* words have the same vowel sound, but when I read my *y* words, I hear different sounds for *y*. So I'm going to sort my words with the *y* endings into two different columns; the long *a* words, and the long *i* words. [*Some students may have long e words, too.*]

- Have students sort the words from their own lists. Circulate around the classroom and have each group or pair describe their method of sorting.

- Bring the class together to reach a consensus about the generalization, for example: *The short vowel sound in words like* mud *is spelled with* u. *A long vowel sound at the end of a word is usually spelled with* y *or a vowel plus* y. Have students write their version on page 42 of the Student Book.

- You might also write the generalization on a sentence strip or poster to display for the duration of the lesson. Leave room for students to add some of their Prove It! words from Day 3.

- Students can preserve their word sorts by gluing the word cards to a separate sheet of paper. Otherwise, they can store their Sorting Boxes. (See page xi in this Teacher's Edition.)

Day 3
Prove It!

Have students review the generalization of words with a short *u* or *y* as a long vowel and find more examples in available materials, such as science books, storybooks, or leveled readers. Be sure that students can read the words and that the words prove the generalization. You may want to adjust the number of words students should find, depending on students' needs. Invite students to share their lists with the class. Keep these lists in a class word bank or chart for future reference.

Day 4
Spelling for Writing

The main goal of this writing assignment is for students to show that they can use the words in a piece of writing. Have students write a description of the outdoors that uses as many spelling and Prove It! words as possible. Before they begin to write, make a list of students' suggestions of things they can write about, for example, stepping in a mud puddle, watching a bug, or hearing a bus go by. If possible, take students outside (or to the window) to get firsthand experiences.

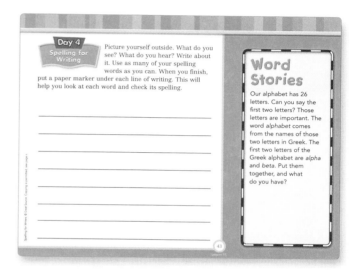

Offer these tips to students:

- Close your eyes and picture an outdoor scene.

- Write some words that describe what you see.

- Use sensory words that help the reader see and hear your scene.

Proofreading Tip One way to help students focus on one line of text at a time is to have them use a marker. Show students how to use a piece of paper as a marker under each line so their eyes can concentrate on the words in just one line at a time.

Word Stories Ask students what they know about the alphabet. Accept any accurate answers. Point out that there are many different kinds of alphabets. Each kind uses symbols to stand for letters. Mention other alphabets, such as sign language or Braille alphabets. Invite students to suggest others (Hebrew or Arabic, for example). Point out that ancient Greece had an alphabet that was like ours in some ways. It had many different symbols to represent the sounds in words. The first two were named *alpha* and *beta*. Our word *alphabet* comes from the names of those letters.

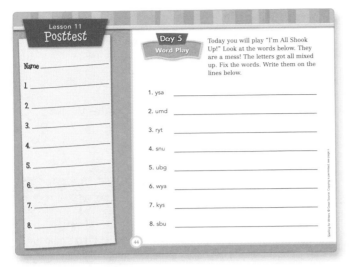

Write the word *red* on the board. Ask a volunteer to read it. Now write *dre* on the board. Ask how it is like *red* and how it is different (same letters, different order). Explain that the letters that spell *red* are all mixed up. To fix the word, someone would have to unscramble the letters. Now write the letters *omp* on the board. Challenge students to unscramble it. Explain that the words on page 44 in their books are also mixed up. Have students then work independently or in pairs or groups to unscramble the words. When they have finished, invite them to read the words aloud.

Posttest Have students tear out the perforated posttest. Students should pair up with their buddies or partners and exchange School Lists (page 41 in the Student Book). Students take turns testing each other on their respective spelling words. Collect the posttest sheets, score them, and record the correct response percentages (Teacher's Edition page 180). Mastery is 6 out of 8 words correct (75%). For students who do not achieve posttest mastery, see page xv in this Teacher's Edition.

Anchor Words After the posttest, have students select one or two anchor words to help them remember the word feature in this lesson. Record the words on the "Anchor Words" poster and refer to them in the Review lesson.

Periodically, check writing samples from your students for transfer of the word features that have been taught. The features for the last three lessons are as follows:

Lesson 9: Short Vowels (*a*, *i*)
Lesson 10: Short Vowels (*e*, *o*)
Lesson 11: Short and Long Vowels (*u*, *y*)

Lesson 12 Long Vowels (silent letter patterns). Sometimes vowel letters make a pattern in which one vowel is long and one is silent, as in *rain*, *read*, and *road*.

Day 1
Pretest and Word Lists

Before Photocopy the Answer Key/ Shopping List page (page 56 in this Teacher's Edition) for each student.

During Say each word in boldface, read the context sentence, and then repeat the word. Have students write the words in the Pretest column on page 45 of the Student Book.

After Distribute to students a copy of the Answer Key/Shopping List page so that they can correct their pretests.

- Students should cross out any misspelled words and write the correct spelling. Words that were correctly spelled can be replaced with words from the Shopping List. Assign a list from which students should choose their words. (See below.)

- Be sure that each student has a list of eight correctly spelled words, which they should copy into the School and At-Home Lists and the Sorting Boxes (page 56).

Pretest context sentences (spelling word in bold):

1. We can go outside after the **rain** stops.
2. I **wait** for my school bus at the corner.
3. My baseball **team** won its last game.
4. Many buses travel on this **road**.
5. That book was fun to **read**.
6. A full **pail** of water is hard to carry.
7. **Each** person may have one sandwich and one dessert.
8. That player is trying to kick the ball into the **goal**.

At-Home List Send the At-Home List home so that families can help their students study the words and features. Several literacy activities are given on the back of the At-Home List: thinking up rhyming words, unscrambling words, and writing words in code.

> **NOTE** The Shopping List provides words below grade level (column 1), words at grade level (column 2), and more challenging words that still have the feature (column 3).

Name _____

Answer Key

1. rain   5. read
2. wait   6. pail
3. team   7. each
4. road   8. goal

Shopping List

nail	hail	aim
tail	paint	brain
eat	beat	heated
oat	float	throat

Sorting Boxes

Day 2
Word Sorting

Have students look at the words carefully. Then have them decide for themselves a way or ways in which they can sort the words (do an open sort). Once they have made their sorts, ask them to say how the words are similar or different. What students say about the words shows you what they understand.

If students have not or cannot decide what the words have in common, model a way to sort all the words. You can use oversized word cards (CD-ROM) or a cut-up transparency (Transparency 11) and overhead to facilitate your model. Use the following Think Aloud with your visuals.

Dear Families,

This week's spelling/word study focuses on long vowel sounds. Help your child learn the words on the back of this letter by doing any of the following activities.

1. Encourage your child to think of words that rhyme with his or her spelling words.

2. Use magnetic letters on your refrigerator to scramble the letters of a spelling word (such as the letters in *read*). Have your child unscramble the letters to spell the word correctly.

3. Make a simple code with your child. Number the alphabet from 1 to 26. Convert several words to numbers and have your child "decode" them.

Spelling for Writers. © Great Source

Day 2
Word Sorting

Listen to the vowel sound in each of your spelling words. Sort your words by the way the vowels sound. Then explain how you sorted the words.

Write Your Generalization _____

_____

_____

Day 3
Prove It!

Find eight more words that prove the generalization that you wrote in the space above.

1._____   5._____
2._____   6._____
3._____   7._____
4._____   8._____

TEACHER'S THINK ALOUD My eye sees that all my spelling cards have two vowels that are beside each other. When I say the words, I notice that some of them have a long *a* sound like in the word *rain*. I see and hear the *a*, but the vowel beside it is silent. I hear a long *e* sound in some of the words. My eye sees *e* and *a*, but I only hear the long *e* sound so the *a* must be silent, like in *read*. In words like *road*, I see an *o* and an *a*. The *o* is long, but the *a* is silent. All my words have a long vowel sound with another vowel beside it. My ear hears long *e*, long *a*, and long *o*, but my eye sees a silent vowel next to the long vowel letter.

- Have students sort the words from their own lists. Circulate around the classroom and have each group or pair describe their method of sorting.

- Help students come up with a generalization. An example is this: *When I sorted my words I discovered that the long vowel sounds of* a, e, *and* o *can be spelled with a silent vowel letter next to them.* Have students write their version on page 46 of the Student Book.

- You might also write the generalization on a sentence strip or poster to display for the duration of the lesson. Leave room for students to add some of their Prove It! words from Day 3.

- Students can preserve their word sorts by gluing the word cards to a separate sheet of paper. Otherwise, they can store their Sorting Boxes. (See page xi in this Teacher's Edition.)

Have students review the generalization and find more examples in available readable materials, such as newspaper, magazines, or storybooks. Be sure students can read the words, and that the words prove the generalization. You may want to adjust the number of words students should find, depending on students' needs. Invite students to share their lists with the class. Keep these lists in a class word bank or chart for future reference.

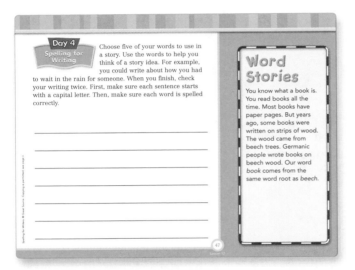

Have students choose five of their words to use in a story. Before students begin to write, have a discussion about stories that are suggested by the words. For example, they might write about waiting in the rain or scoring a goal for the team. Make a list of ideas that students can choose from. If there is time, have students read their stories aloud.

Proofreading Tip Teach students to look *for* something when they proofread because careful proofreaders look for only one thing at a time. This means that students will have to check through their writing more than once. For example, they might look first to be sure that all the sentences have a capital letter at the beginning. Then they might check for spelling.

Word Stories Ask students to describe a book. Point out that ancient people were writing long before modern books existed. Many ancient people wrote on strips of wood or bark. One group of ancient people used wood from beech trees. Their word for beech tree was *buche*. The modern word *book* comes from that. You may also wish to point out that another group of people wrote on tree bark. These people lived in Rome. Their word for bark was *liber*. The modern word *library* comes from that ancient Roman word.

Day 5
Word Play and Posttest

Choose one word from this week's list, such as *throat*. Ask students how they would define the word. Accept any reasonable answers. Explain that now they will have a chance to write their own definitions. If they can, they should try to illustrate each definition with a picture. Tell them that illustrations help readers understand definitions. Demonstrate this by showing an illustration from a children's dictionary. Have students then work in pairs or groups to complete the activity. When they have finished, invite them to read the definitions aloud and display their illustrations.

Lesson 12
Posttest

Name _____

1. _____
2. _____
3. _____
4. _____
5. _____
6. _____
7. _____
8. _____

Day 5
Word Play

A dictionary tells the meaning of words. Pick three of your words. Write a definition for each word. Remember, pictures can help readers understand a word. You can add pictures to your dictionary.

Posttest   Have students tear out the perforated posttest. Students should pair up with their buddies or partners and exchange School Lists (page 45 in the Student Book). Students take turns testing each other on their respective spelling words. Collect the posttest sheets, score them, and record the correct response percentages (Teacher's Edition page 180). Mastery is 6 out of 8 words correct (75%). For students who do not achieve posttest mastery, see page xv in this Teacher's Edition.

Anchor Words After the posttest, have students select one or two anchor words to help them remember the word feature in this lesson. Record the words on the "Anchor Words" poster and refer to them in the Review lesson.

Lesson 13

Long Vowels (*i, u*). The sound of long *i* can be spelled with *i* alone (*find*), *i* plus the *e* marker (*life*), or *y* (*July*). The sound of long *u* can be spelled with *u* alone or with *u* plus the *e* marker.

Day 1
Pretest and Word Lists

Before Photocopy the Answer Key/Shopping List page (page 61 in this Teacher's Edition) for each student.

During Say each word in boldface, read the context sentence, and then repeat the word. Have students write the words in the Pretest column on page 49 of the Student Book.

After Distribute to students a copy of the Answer Key/Shopping List page so that they can correct their pretests.

- Students should cross out any misspelled words and write the correct spelling. Words that were correctly spelled can be replaced with words from the Shopping List. Assign a list from which students should choose their words. (See below.)

- Be sure that each student has a list of eight correctly spelled words, which they should copy into the School and At-Home Lists and the Sorting Boxes (page 61).

Pretest context sentences (spelling word in bold):

1. My teacher is a **nice** person.
2. I have spent my whole **life** in this apartment.
3. My granddad **used** a hearing aid to hear better.
4. I know the **tune** to that song but not the words.
5. I saw a picture of someone riding on a **mule**.
6. What **kind** of sandwich did you bring?
7. I need to **find** a pen or a pencil.
8. The month of May comes before **June**.

At-Home List Send the At-Home List home so that families can help their students study the words and features. Several literacy activities are given on the back of the At-Home List: alphabetizing the spelling words, using letters cut from newspaper and magazines to spell words, finding shorter words within spelling words, and writing the words in shaving cream or liquid soap.

> **NOTE** The Shopping List provides words below grade level (column 1), words at grade level (column 2), and more challenging words that have the feature (column 3).

Name _____

Shopping List

bike	dime	knife
ice	tube	tries
July	rude	music
true	rule	bluer

Sorting Boxes

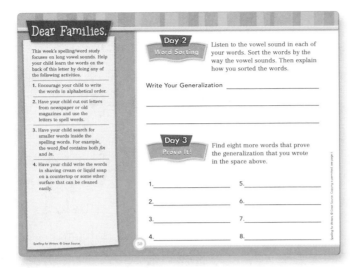

Day 2
Word Sorting

Have students look at the words carefully. Then have them decide for themselves a way or ways in which they can sort the words (do an open sort). Once they have made their sorts, ask them to say how the words are similar or different. What students say about the words shows you what they understand.

If students have not or cannot decide what the words have in common, model a way to sort all the words. You can use over-sized word cards (CD-ROM) or a cut-up transparency (Transparency 12) and overhead to facilitate your model. Use the following Think Aloud with your visuals.

> **TEACHER'S THINK ALOUD** When I read my words out loud, my ear hears that sees that all my spelling words have long vowel sounds and I can put them into two categories: long *i* and long *u*. I know that when the vowel letter *e* is at the end of the word it often makes the vowel before the consonant sound long, as in the word *life*. The words *kind* and *find* are spelled with only the vowel letter *i*, and in *July* the long *i* is spelled with *y*.

- Have students sort the words from their own lists. Circulate around the classroom and have each group or pair describe their method of sorting.

- Bring the class together to reach a consensus about the generalization. Example: *I sorted my words and I discovered they all had long vowel sounds. One category had a long* u *spelled* u *consonant* e. *The other category had long* i *spelled with* i *consonant* e, i *by itself, or the letter* y. (Only students who chose *July* from the Shopping List will have the latter.)

- Have students write their version of the generalization on page 50 of the Student Book.

- You might also write the generalization on a sentence strip or poster to display for the duration of the lesson. Leave room for students to add some of their Prove It! words from Day 3.

- Students can preserve their word sorts by gluing the word cards to a separate sheet of paper. Otherwise, they can store their Sorting Boxes. (See page xi in this Teacher's Edition.)

Day 3

Prove It!

Have students review the generalization and find more examples in available texts, such as textbooks, mystery stories, calendars, or other appropriate reading materials. Be sure students can read the words, and that the words prove the fit the pattern. You may want to adjust the number of words students should find, depending on students' needs. Invite students to share their lists with the class. Keep these lists in a class word bank or chart for future reference.

Day 4

Spelling for Writing

Have students write about what they like to do in the month of June. Before students begin to write, help them come up with ideas. Make a list of ideas for students to choose from. Encourage students to use as many of their spelling words and Prove It! words as possible.

Offer these tips for writing:

- Close your eyes to picture what you like to do in June.

- Include details to help the reader picture what you like to do.

- Draw a picture first, if that will help.

Proofreading Tip Remind students that reading out loud is a good idea when proofreading because it slows them down and it helps them hear when words may have been left out.

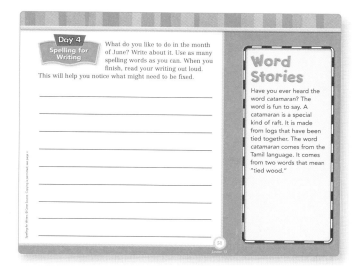

Word Stories Ask students if they have ever seen a real boat or raft, especially a sailboat that is a catamaran. If so, have them describe it. Ask what materials boats and rafts are made of (e.g., wood, metal, rubber, or fiberglass). Explain that one type of raft is called a catamaran. It is made from a pair of long logs that are tied together with other logs. Discuss why this would be better than just one log. Then explain that the word *catamaran* comes from the Tamil language. Many people in India speak this language. *Catamaran* comes from a Tamil word that means "tied wood" or "wood that is tied together." Ask students if they would like to ride on a catamaran some day. Have them give reasons for their answers.

Have students choose five of their words and fingerspell them. Students will use the American Sign Language alphabet chart shown on Student Book page 52 to form each letter. Have students practice and then fingerspell to a buddy, so they can try to figure out each other's words.

Posttest Have students tear out the perforated posttest. Students should pair up with their buddies or partners and exchange School Lists (page 49 in the Student Book). Students take turns testing each other on their respective spelling words. Collect the posttest sheets, score them, and record the correct response percentages (Teacher's Edition page 180). Mastery is 6 out of 8 words correct (75%). For students who do not achieve posttest mastery, see page xv in this Teacher's Edition.

Anchor Words After the posttest, have students select one or two anchor words to help them remember the word feature in this lesson. Record the words on the "Anchor Words" poster and refer to them in the Review lesson.

Lesson 14 Consonant Digraphs (*ch, th*). Two consonants can come together to make a single sound, as in *child*.

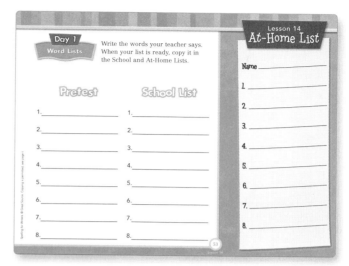

Day 1
Pretest and Word Lists

Before Photocopy the Answer Key/ Shopping List page (page 66 in this Teacher's Edition) for each student.

During Say each word in boldface, read the context sentence, and then repeat the word. Have students write the words in the Pretest column on page 53 of the Student Book.

After Distribute to students a copy of the Answer Key/Shopping List page so that they can correct their pretests.

- Students should cross out any misspelled words and write the correct spelling. Words that were correctly spelled can be replaced with words from the Shopping List. Assign a list from which students should choose their words. (See below.)

- Be sure that each student has a list of eight correctly spelled words, which they should copy into the School and At-Home Lists and the Sorting Boxes (page 66).

Pretest context sentences (spelling word in bold):

1. Please come **with** me.
2. One **child** is absent from school today.
3. I know **the** answer.
4. I win if I **reach** the finish line first.
5. I love **that** song!
6. The gorilla pounded its **chest**.
7. We eat **lunch** at noon.
8. **Both** of us can sit at the table.

At-Home List Send the At-Home List home so that families can help their students study the words and features. Several literacy activities are given on the back of the At-Home List: making scrambled word puzzles, providing the missing *th* or *ch* to spell words, and translating letters of words into telephone keypad numbers.

> **NOTE** The Shopping List provides words below grade level (column 1), words at grade level (column 2), and more challenging words that have the *feature* (column 3).

Name _____

Shopping List

thin	them	worth
this	bath	thinking
chin	rich	itchy
chat	cheese	chase

Sorting Boxes

Day 2
Word Sorting

Have students look at the words carefully. Then have them decide for themselves a way or ways in which they can sort the words (do an open sort). Once they have made their sorts, ask them to say how the words are similar or different. What students say about the words shows you what they understand.

If students have not or cannot decide what the words have in common, model a way to sort all the words. You can use oversized word cards (CD-ROM) or a cut-up transparency (Transparency 13) and overhead to facilitate your model. Use the following Think Aloud with your visuals.

Dear Families,

This week's spelling/word study focuses on the sounds represented by *th* and *ch*. Help your child learn the words on the back of this letter by doing any of the following activities.

1. Help your child make scrambled word puzzles. Show him or her how to scramble the letters of each word and list the scrambled words in a column. Next to the column, have your child draw lines to write on. See how many of the words you can unscramble and write on the line.

2. Write your child's spelling words but leave out the *th* or *ch* in each one. Have your child fill in the missing letters and then say each word out loud.

3. Help your child translate words into numbers using a telephone keypad. For example, the word *the* would become 8-4-3. Your child can then "spell" words using keypad numbers.

Spelling for Writers. © Great Source.

Day 2
Word Sorting

What do you see when you look at your words? What do you hear when you say your words? Sort your words in a way that makes sense. Then write how the words are the same or different.

Write Your Generalization _____

_____

Day 3
Prove It!

Find eight more words that prove the generalization that you wrote in the space above.

1. _____ 5. _____
2. _____ 6. _____
3. _____ 7. _____
4. _____ 8. _____

> **TEACHER'S THINK ALOUD** What do I notice when I look at my words? What do I notice when I say my words out loud? I see that all the words have the letter *h* in them, but I hear two different sounds. When the *t* is next to the *h*, I hear the /th/ or /th/ sound, as in *thin* or *that*, which doesn't sound like a *t* or an *h*. When the *c* is next to the *h*, I hear the /ch/ sound, as in *chest*, which doesn't sound like a *c* or an *h*. I will sort my words into two categories.

- Have students sort the words from their own lists. Circulate around the classroom and have each group or pair describe their method of sorting.

- Bring the class together to reach a consensus about the generalization, for example: *When* t *is paired with* h *it makes a new sound, and when* c *is paired with* h *it makes a new sound.* Have students write their version on page 54 of the Student Book.

- You might also write the generalization on a sentence strip or poster to display for the duration of the lesson. Leave room for students to add some of their Prove It! words from Day 3.

- Students can preserve their word sorts by gluing the word cards to a separate sheet of paper. Otherwise, they can store their Sorting Boxes. (See page xi in this Teacher's Edition.)

Have students review the generalization and find more examples in available readable materials, such as leveled books, poems, school announcements, or other appropriate reading materials. Be sure students can read the words and that the words fit the pattern. You may want to adjust the number of words students should find, depending on students' needs. Invite students to share their lists with the class. Keep these lists in a class word bank or chart for future reference.

Day 3
Prove It!

Day 4
Spelling for Writing

Have students use spelling words and Prove It! words to write about lunch. They can write about any aspect of lunch that appeals to them. Suggest that they look at their word list to figure out what to write. Some students might benefit from drawing a picture before they write.

Offer these tips for writing:

- Ask yourselves some questions: What do I like to eat for lunch? With whom do I eat lunch? Was there something funny or interesting that happened during a lunch?

- Use some words that will help your readers see, hear, and even taste the action in your writing! For example, "When I bit into my apple, I heard a loud crunch!"

- Draw a picture first, if it will help.

Proofreading Tip On a large piece of text, demonstrate for the students how to touch every word with a finger or pencil so that the eyes concentrate on one word at a time.

Word Stories Ask students what they know about spiders. Accept any reasonable answers. Point out, if necessary, that spiders have eight legs. Explain, too, that different kinds of spiders live in different places. If possible, show a picture of a tarantula and identify it. A dictionary may have an illustration. Then explain that the word *tarantula* comes from the name of a town in Italy. The town is Taranto. Remind students that they learned about other words that came from the names of places: *bologna* and *frankfurter.* You may wish to point out that years ago, people believed that the bite of this spider made people want to dance. Today, there is a dance called the *tarantella.* That word, too, comes from the name of the town Taranto.

Day 5
Word Play and Posttest

Have students choose five of their words and fingerspell them. Students will use the American Sign Language alphabet chart show on Student Book page 56 to form each letter. Have students practice and then fingerspell to a buddy, so they can try to figure out each other's words.

Posttest Have students tear out the perforated posttest. Students should pair up with their buddies or partners and exchange School Lists (page 53 in the Student Book). Students take turns testing each other on their respective spelling words. Collect the posttest sheets, score them, and record the correct response percentages (Teacher's Edition page 180). Mastery is 6 out of 8 words correct (75%). For students who do not achieve posttest mastery, see page xv in this Teacher's Edition.

Anchor Words After the posttest, have students select one or two anchor words to help them remember the word feature in this lesson. Record the words on the "Anchor Words" poster and refer to them in the Review lesson.

Periodically, check writing samples from your students for transfer of the word features that have been taught. The features for the last three lessons are as follows:

Lesson 12: Long Vowels (*silent letter patterns*)
Lesson 13: Long Vowels (*i, u*)
Lesson 14: Consonant Digraphs (*ch, th*)

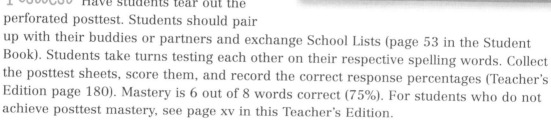

Lesson 15 Consonant Blends. When a consonant comes before an *l* or an *r*, the sounds are blended together (*free, blue*).

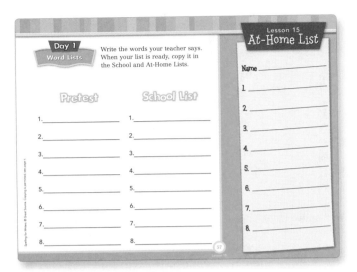

Day 1
Pretest and Word Lists

Before Photocopy the Answer Key/ Shopping List page (page 71 in this Teacher's Edition) for each student.

During Say each word in boldface, read the context sentence, and then repeat the word. Have students write the words in the Pretest column on page 57 of the Student Book.

After Distribute to students a copy of the Answer Key/Shopping List page so that they can correct their pretests.

- Students should cross out any misspelled words and write the correct spelling. Words that were correctly spelled can be replaced with words from the Shopping List. Assign a list from which students should choose their words. (See below.)

- Be sure that each student has a list of eight correctly spelled words, which they should copy into the School and At-Home Lists and the Sorting Boxes (page 71).

Pretest context sentences (spelling word in bold):

1. I like to sit with a ***friend*** at lunch.
2. The sunlight made me ***blink*** several times.
3. This pen has ***black*** ink.
4. Will you ***fry*** that egg or scramble it?
5. Move away ***from*** the window.
6. My mother has ***blue*** eyes.
7. Cut a slice of cheese off that big ***block***.
8. Is that ***free*** or is there some cost?

At-Home List Send the At-Home List home so that families can help their students study the words and features. Several literacy activities are given on the back of the At-Home List: hunting for spelling words in print media, writing the words without vowels, and making up riddles.

> **NOTE** The Shopping List provides words below grade level (column 1), words at grade level (column 2), and more challenging words that have the feature (column 3).

Name _____

Shopping List

frog	fright	frame
Friday	frown	freeze
blind	blew	bloom
blot	blood	bleacher

Sorting Boxes

Day 2
Word Sorting

Dear Families,

This week's spelling/word study focuses on the consonant pairs *fr* and *bl.* Help your child learn the words on the back of this letter by doing any of the following activities.

1. With your child, look through newspapers and magazines to find words from the list. You should be able to find *from, free,* and *blue,* for example, and perhaps others. Have your child cut out examples and attach them to a sheet of paper.

2. Have your child write the words without using any vowels. He or she should use either a star or a question mark to replace each vowel. See how many of those words you can guess.

3. Have your child make up riddles that either contain the spelling words or have them as the answer. For example, "What is *black* and white and red all over?" (a blushing zebra)

Spelling for Writers. © Great Source.

Day 2
Word Sorting

What do you see when you look at your words? What do you hear when you say your words? Sort your words in a way that makes sense. Then write how the words are the same or different.

Write Your Generalization _____

_____

_____

Day 3
Prove It!

Find eight more words that prove the generalization that you wrote in the space above.

1._____ 5._____

2._____ 6._____

3._____ 7._____

4._____ 8._____

Spelling for Writers. © Great Source. Copying is permitted; see page x.

58

Have students look at the words carefully. Then have them decide for themselves a way or ways in which they can sort the words (do an open sort). Once they have made their sorts, ask them to say how the words are similar or different. What students say about the words shows you what they understand.

If students have not or cannot decide what the words have in common, model a way to sort all the words. You can use oversized word cards (CD-ROM) or a cut-up transparency (Transparency 14) and overhead to facilitate your model. Use the following Think Aloud with your visuals.

> **TEACHER'S THINK ALOUD** I know I need to use my brain, ears, and eyes when I read these cards. All of my spelling cards have something in common. So, I am going to think and look and listen. I notice that all my words have a pair of consonants at the beginning. There are two different pairs. They are *fr* as in *free*, or *bl* as in *black*. I hear both consonants blend together, but they keep their own consonant sounds.

- Have students sort the words from their own lists. Circulate around the classroom and have each group or pair describe their method of sorting.

- Bring the class together to reach a consensus about the generalization, for example: *Sometimes consonants blend together and keep their own consonant sounds.* Have students write their version on page 58 of the Student Book.

- Tell students that when they hear a consonant blend in a word, they should remember to write all the letters in the blend.

- You might also write the generalization on a sentence strip or poster to display for the duration of the lesson. Leave room for students to add some of their Prove It! words from Day 3.

- Students can preserve their word sorts by gluing the word cards to a separate sheet of paper. Otherwise, they can store their Sorting Boxes. (See page xi in this Teacher's Edition.)

Day 3
Prove It!

Have students review the generalization and find more examples in available readable materials, such as science or math books, storybooks, or newspaper fliers. Be sure students can read the words and that the words prove the generalization. You may want to adjust the number of words students should find, depending on students' needs. Invite students to share their lists with the class. Keep these lists in a class word bank or chart for future reference.

Day 4
Spelling for Writing

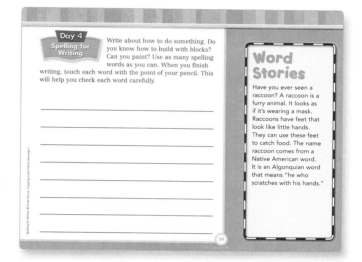

Students are asked to do some how-to (expository) writing to explain something they know how to do. Before students begin to write, help them come up with some ideas for writing. They should use as many spelling words and Prove It! words as they can.

Offer these tips for writing:

- Expository writing explains something.

- Write about something that you know well.

- Write the details in the order that you would do them.

- Use time words like *first, next,* and *then* to make your writing clear.

Proofreading Tip Authors are good at writing, but proofreaders are good at proofreading! Often it is easier to proofread someone else's writing because the reader is less familiar with the text and errors tend to stand out. Have students exchange their papers with a buddy and proofread each other's writing. Emphasize that all comments should be respectful and helpful.

Word Stories Have students describe a raccoon, if they can. If they cannot, display a picture of one. Then explain that raccoons live wild in North America. Native Americans were very familiar with this animal. They knew its habits and knew that it uses its paws like hands. The word *raccoon* comes from an Algonquian word for this animal. It means "he who scratches with his hands." Discuss why this is an appropriate name. You may wish to mention that *skunk* is another word from the Algonquian language. It means "spray of smelly water."

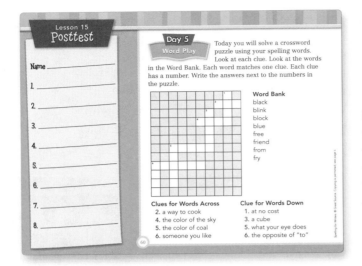

Day 5
Word Play and Posttest

Show students the crossword puzzle and demonstrate how to match the clues with the puzzle. Ask a volunteer to find the word that belongs with the first clue. Then ask another where she or he would write that word in the puzzle. Have students work in pairs or groups to complete the puzzle. Afterwards, have them read their answers aloud.

Posttest Have students tear out the perforated posttest. Students should pair up with their buddies or partners and exchange School Lists (page 57 in the Student Book). Students take turns testing each other on their respective spelling words. Collect the posttest sheets, score them, and record the correct response percentages (Teacher's Edition page 180). Mastery is 6 out of 8 words correct (75%). For students who do not achieve posttest mastery, see page xv in this Teacher's Edition.

Anchor Words After the posttest, have students select one or two anchor words to help them remember the word feature in this lesson. Record the words on the "Anchor Words" poster and refer to them in the Review lesson.

Day 1
Pretest and
Word Lists

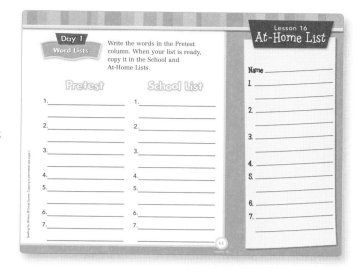

Before There are three options for selecting the pretest words. Choose the one most appropriate for your students.

1. Have students think of words that fit the spelling patterns and write them.

2. Use the words that you and your class collected on the "Anchor Words" poster.

3. Use the examples given on page 76.

If you will dictate the words, either from the "Anchor Words" poster or from page 76, make an answer key by writing the words on a copy of Copy Master 1. Photocopy the filled-in answer key page for each student.

During Announce each word feature on page 76. As you say each feature, also state the generalization and give the words or ask students to think of words. Students will write one or two words for each feature on page 61 of the Student Book.

After If you dictated words, distribute a copy of the answer key so that students can self-correct their pretests. Otherwise, correct students' pretests.

- For any word that students got correct, send them back to the lesson for that feature to select a word from their Prove It! List they want to learn to spell.

- Be sure that each student has a list of correctly spelled words, which they should copy into the School and At-Home Lists and the Sorting Boxes (use Copy Master 1 for the Sorting Boxes).

At-Home List Send the At-Home List home so that families can use the following activities with their children: writing words using different colors for long and short vowel sounds, spelling words using water on a brown paper bag, and having a word hunt.

Word Features and Generalizations

1. **Short Vowels (*a, i*).** A word spelled with a consonant-vowel-consonant (CVC) pattern usually has a short vowel sound (*bag, six*). (*Lesson 9*)

2. **Short Vowels (*e, o*).** A word spelled with a consonant-vowel-consonant (CVC) pattern usually has a short vowel sound (*fox, ten*). (*Lesson 10*)

3. **Short and Long Vowels (*u, y*).** The short *u* sound is spelled with *u* in *sun*. The long sounds of *a, i,* and *e* can be spelled with *y* or a vowel plus *y*. (*way*) (*Lesson 11*)

4. **Long Vowels (silent letter patterns).** Sometimes vowel letters make a pattern in which one vowel is long and one is silent, as in *rain*. (*Lesson 12*)

5. **Long Vowels (*i, u*).** The long sound of a vowel can be spelled with the vowel alone, the vowel plus the *e* marker (*life*), or *y* (*July*). (*Lesson 13*)

6. **Consonant Digraphs (*ch, th*).** Two consonants can come together to make a single sound, as in *child*. (*Lesson 14*)

7. **Consonant Blends.** When a consonant comes before *l* or *r*, the sounds are blended together (*free, blue*). (*Lesson 15*)

Word Sorting

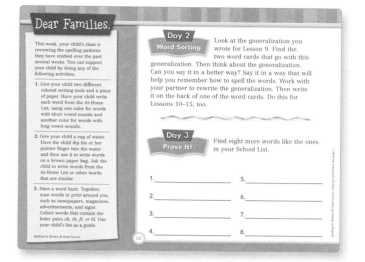

Today students will revisit the generalizations they wrote for Lessons 9–15. They will read them and then decide if they could be stated more clearly.

- Have students cut apart the Sorting Boxes to create word cards for this activity (Copy Master 1).

- Have them form pairs and turn to page 34 of their Student Books.

- Both students should read the generalization they wrote for Lesson 9 and identify the two word cards that relate to this generalization. Then they should ask themselves if the generalization is clear. Could it be stated in a way that would be more helpful in remembering how to spell the words?

- You might work through the first generalization with the class to show students how to clarify and improve the wording.

- Students should then write the best version of the generalization on the back of a relevant word card and move on to the next generalization (Lesson 10).

As a closing step, have students work in pairs to sort their words into groups that make sense. Circulate through the room to talk with students about their word sorts. Students' explanations of their sorts tell you what they understand about how words work.

After students revisit and revise several generalizations for this lesson's review, send them off to find in readable materials more examples that prove as many of the generalizations as possible to be true. Provide appropriate reading materials, such as storybooks, poetry books, newspapers, and textbooks. Be sure that students can read the words they find and that their words prove each generalization. Adjust the amount and kind of reading material students will use as well as the number of words they should find, according to their needs. Invite students to share their lists with the class. Keep these lists in a class word bank or chart for future reference.

Day 3
Prove It!

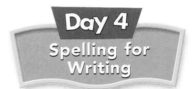

Day 4
Spelling for Writing

Although students should write their stories independently, they might first work with partners to brainstorm story ideas. Encourage them to use as many spelling words as possible in their stories, including words from the word hunt. Many times, nouns and verbs may suggest ideas for stories and characters—for example, the words *mule* and *oat* might suggest a story about a hungry animal.

Proofreading Tip Ask students to state how reading and proofreading are different. (When you proofread, your eyes have to move slowly so that you can look at every letter in a word.) Suggest that students touch their pencil point to each word or letter in a word so that their eyes look at all the letters.

Word Stories Ask if any students can describe or draw a bagel. If so, have a volunteer do so. If a student has only described a bagel, draw one the board: it is shaped like a doughnut. Ask how this is like a ring (round, hole in the center). The word *bagel* came from a Yiddish word, meaning "ring." Point out that *lox* (smoked salmon) is another word from Yiddish. If students are unfamiliar with Yiddish, you may wish to explain that it is a language originally used in European Jewish communities. Yiddish is based on German but written with Hebrew characters.

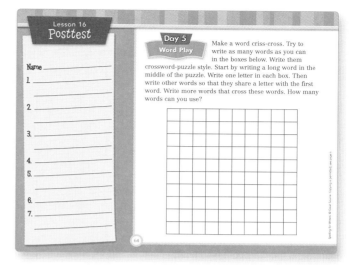

Show students a crossword puzzle, such as one found in most daily newspapers. Show how the words interlock. Review the directions on page 64 of the Student Book and make sure students understand how to use the grid to make their own word criss-crosses. Explain that this is how people begin to create crossword puzzles. They first create word criss-crosses. Then they number the words and write clues.

Encourage students to try to use as many words as possible. After they have completed their puzzles, have them compare them with those of their partners.

Review Activities Other activities that students can do to review the words include the following:

- Have students choose a set of Sorting Boxes from a previous lesson and time themselves when they sort the cards. Students should sort them several times to see whether their sorting time gets faster. (Copy Masters of the pretest words can be found in the Transparencies and Copy Masters folder. Or, generate word cards from the CD-ROM.)

- Students can use their review list in a Word Play activity from a previous lesson, such as a word-find puzzle, or to make another word criss-cross, as in this lesson.

- Generate a practice activity from the CD-ROM.

Posttest Have students carefully tear out the posttest form on Student Book page 64. Students should pair up with their buddies or partners and exchange School Lists (page 61 in the Student Book). Students take turns testing each other on their respective spelling words. Collect the posttest sheets and score them. Mastery is 10 out of 12, or 80%. For students who do not achieve posttest mastery, see page xv in this Teacher's Edition.

Lesson 17 Benchmark Assessment.

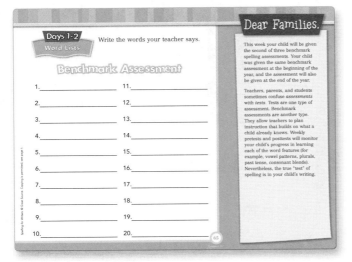

Days 1-2
Word Lists

Before Have students locate page 65 in the Student Book on which they will record the spelling words. This benchmark assessment is the second of three opportunities for you to monitor each student's growth. There are no standards for mastery in the benchmark assessments. Rather, they are informative pieces for instructional planning.

During Say each word in boldface (page 81) aloud. The word features are identified in parentheses for your information. These words were specifically chosen because they represent grade-level words for a given feature. If you substituted other words Lesson 1, use them here. It is recommended that this assessment be administered over two to five days, in short intervals, in order to best meet the needs of your students and to avoid student fatigue. On Days 3-5, if the assessment is still ongoing, students can continue with the other activities after you administer a small portion of the assessment.

After Interpret students' responses, analyzing first their successes in spelling a word that meets the word feature criterion and then taking a hard look at where they may have miscued, perhaps recalling a different word feature and misapplying it. We strongly encourage you to analyze students' responses not for errors but for insights into the strategies that students employed to spell each word. This is your window into their thinking about the language. You can use these insights to adapt your teaching so that it improves students' abilities to choose successful spelling strategies.

We suggest you do not mark in the Student Book. A record sheet is provided (see page 179 in this Teacher's Edition). This records the features and allows you to document growth for each student. It is important for students not to see the markings, so simply transfer any attempts to the record sheet. This reinforces the understanding that *Spelling for Writers* developmentally supports the spelling strategies that students bring to their writing, rather than focusing on mastery of whole words. As you will notice, the students' profile easily documents growth.

Benchmark Assessment This is the second of three Benchmark Assessments. The Benchmark Assessments provide a record of students' spelling from this year and can be noted in a portfolio and passed along to next year's teachers.

1. **late** (short and long vowel *a*)
2. **yes** (short and long vowel *e*)
3. **big** (short and long vowel *i*)
4. **toe** (short and long vowel *o*)
5. **use** (short and long vowel *u*)
6. **try** (long vowel *y*)
7. **man** (short vowels *a, i*)
8. **mop** (short vowels *e, o*)
9. **dust** (short vowel *u*, long vowel *y*)
10. **keep** (long vowels *a, e, o*)
11. **ice** (long vowels *i, u*)
12. **child** (digraphs)
13. **free** (consonants blends)
14. **kick** (final consonants)
15. **stars** (plural -*s*)
16. **foxes** (plural -*es*)
17. **men** (irregular plurals)
18. **know** (silent consonant patterns)
19. **high** (silent vowel patterns)
20. **rain** (silent vowel patterns)
21. **told** (irregular past tense)
22. **wrapped** (past tense -*ed*)
23. **thank** (preconsonant nasals)
24. **apple** (short and long vowel *a*)
25. **letter** (short and long vowel *e*)
26. **inside** (short and long vowel *i*)
27. **opening** (short and long vowel *o*)
28. **cuter** (short and long vowel *u*)

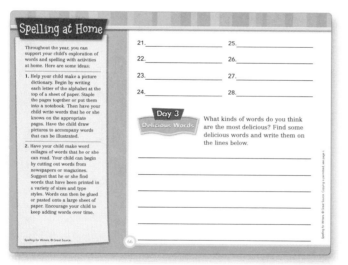

21._____ 25._____
22._____ 26._____
23._____ 27._____
24._____ 28._____

Day 3
Delicious Words

What kinds of words do you think are the most delicious? Find some delicious words and write them on the lines below.

_____
_____
_____
_____

Letter to the Families

Students may carefully remove the perforated section of page 65 in the Student Book and take it home to share with their families. It includes a note to families explaining the benchmark assessments and how they will be used to shape instruction. On the back of this note are several At-Home activities that families can use to support their students' learning. These activities include making a picture dictionary and making word collages.

After students have completed today's benchmark assessment, tell them that they are going to go on a word hunt. Tell them that they will look for words they would call "delicious"—words that are fun, descriptive, or vivid; words that help them imagine how something looks, feels, tastes, smells, or sounds. For example, if you were reading *Charlotte's Web* to your class, you might note wonderful phrases like "a barn that is perfumed with rotten egg" or "he felt radiant and happy." Talk with students about words that could make their writing come alive, like *perfumed* or *radiant*. Provide appropriate materials for the word hunt, such as picture books and children's magazines. Students should write their words in the on page 66 of the Student Book. Keep an on-going list on the "Delicious Words" poster as a resource of terrific words for students to use in their writing.

What do you think about spelling? What have you learned about spelling so far this year? Write a few sentences that tell your ideas about spelling. When you are finished, touch each word with your pencil point. Make sure the letters are correct for each word.

Word Stories

Many words that we use every day come from other languages. For example, do you know someone with a baby? A baby wears a diaper. The word *diaper* comes from the Greek language. The Greek word means "white."

After students have completed today's portion of the benchmark assessment, make sure they understand the writing assignment. Students are to write about their progress as spellers. Ask them to think about what they have learned, what they know about spelling, their opinion of spelling, and so forth. Students' answers will tell you their attitude about spelling and offer you insight as to how they see themselves as spellers.

Proofreading Tip Explain to students that proofreading is a special kind of reading that writers do to make sure that their writing has no errors. Proofreading must be done slowly and carefully.

Word Stories On Student Book page 67, students are told that the word *diaper* comes from the Greek word for *white*. Talk about why this makes sense. (A diaper can be made of white cloth or, now, white synthetic materials.) On Student Book page 68, students are asked to find out which language gave us the words *blanket*, *denim*, and *mitten*. Notice that both *diaper* and *blanket* come from words that mean "white." (*Blanket* is based on the French word for white, *blanc*. *Denim* is from the French words "de Nimes," which means "of or from Nimes." Nimes is a town in France. *Mitten* is from an old French word that meant "cat's caress.")

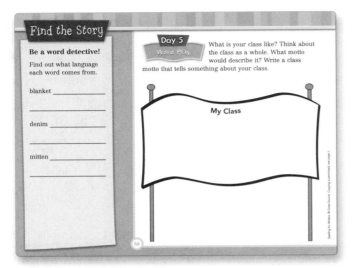

Find the Story

Be a word detective!

Find out what language each word comes from.

blanket _____

_____

denim _____

_____

mitten _____

_____

Students are to think of words and phrases that describe their class. Hold a brainstorming session to help students think of such descriptors. Then students are to come up with a motto that describes the class. Students can work to make one big banner for the whole class, they can work in a small group or with a partner, or they can work independently.

Lesson 18 Consonants (final k, ck).

At the end of a word, the sound of /k/ can be spelled with k or ck, as in *took* and *back*.

Day 1
Pretest and Word Lists

Day 1 Word Lists

Write the words your teacher says. When your list is ready, copy it in the School and At-Home Lists.

Pretest

1._____
2._____
3._____
4._____
5._____
6._____
7._____
8._____

School List

1._____
2._____
3._____
4._____
5._____
6._____
7._____
8._____

Lesson 18 At-Home List

Name _____

1._____
2._____
3._____
4._____
5._____
6._____
7._____
8._____

Before Photocopy the Answer Key/ Shopping List page (page 86 in this Teacher's Edition) for each student.

During Say each word in boldface, read the context sentence, and then repeat the word. Have students write the words in the Pretest column on page 69 of the Student Book.

After Distribute to students a copy of the Answer Key/Shopping List page so that they can correct their pretests.

- Students should cross out any misspelled words and write the correct spelling. Words that were correctly spelled can be replaced with words from the Shopping List. Assign the column from which students should choose their words. (See below.)

- Be sure that each student has a list of eight correctly spelled words, which they should copy into the School and At-Home Lists and the Sorting Boxes (page 86).

Pretest context sentences (spelling word in bold):

1. Someone must **cook** this meat before we can eat it.
2. Yes, I **took** my homework to school.
3. Please **pack** your own lunch today.
4. The **duck** made a nest by the lake.
5. The **bark** on that tree is white and black.
6. The clown had a red dot on each **cheek**.
7. Look in the **back** of the book for answers.
8. I stayed home from school because I was **sick**.

At-Home List Send the At-Home List home so that families can help their students study the words and features. Several literacy activities are given on the back of the At-Home List: drawing outline boxes around each letter of spelling words, finding words in a word chain, identifying words that have been written on a person's palm or back, and writing words crossword-puzzle style.

> **NOTE** The Shopping List provides words below grade level (column 1), words at grade level (column 2), and more challenging words that have the feature (column 3).

Name _____

Answer Key

1. cook	**5.** bark
2. took	**6.** cheek
3. pack	**7.** back
4. duck	**8.** sick

Shopping List

black	stack	junk
pick	track	stink
dock	pink	luck
book	shook	shock

Sorting Boxes

Day 2
Word Sorting

Have students look at the words carefully. Then have them decide for themselves a way or ways in which they can sort the words (do an open sort). Once they have made their sorts, ask them to say how the words are similar or different. What students say about the words shows you what they understand.

If students have not or cannot decide what the words have in common, model a way to sort all the words. You can use oversized word cards (CD-ROM) or a cut-up transparency (Transparency 15) and overhead to facilitate your model. Use the following Think Aloud with your visuals.

> **Dear Families,**
>
> This week's spelling/word study focuses on words that end with *k* or *ck*. Help your child learn the words on the back of this letter by doing any of the following activities.
>
> 1. Have your child write three or four words on lined paper. Then have him or her draw boxes around each letter. Tall letters should have boxes that are taller than vowels. Letters that hang below the line should have boxes that hang below the line. Vowels should have square boxes.
> 2. Write all the words from the back of this letter in a word chain, with no spaces between them. Have your child find and circle each word in the chain.
> 3. Write words on your child's back or open palm with your finger and see if your child can identify the word.
> 4. Have your child write pairs of words crossword-puzzle style, so that they cross at a letter they have in common.
>
> *Spelling for Writers © Great Source.*
>
> **Day 2 Word Sorting** Listen to the sound at the end of each word. How is this sound spelled? Sort your words. Then explain how you sorted the words.
>
> Write Your Generalization _____
>
> _____
>
> _____
>
> **Day 3 Prove It!** Find eight more words that prove the generalization that you wrote in the space above.
>
> 1._____ 5._____
> 2._____ 6._____
> 3._____ 7._____
> 4._____ 8._____

TEACHER'S THINK ALOUD When I look at my words, I notice that they all end in the letter *k*. Some of my words have a *c* before the *k*, like the word *sick*. My eye sees the *ck*, but I only hear /k/. I can sort my words into two categories, the words that end in *ck* and the words that end in *k*. I'm wondering why some words have a *c* and the others don't. I notice that all the *ck* words have a short vowel sound. So, now I will read out loud the words that end in just *k*. Interesting, these words have a different vowel sound that is not short.

- Have students sort the words from their own lists. Circulate around the classroom and have each group or pair describe their method of sorting.

- Bring the class together to reach a consensus about the generalization. An example is this: *The vowel sound that comes before* ck *is usually short, and the vowel that comes just before* k *is usually not short.* Have students write their version on page 70 of the Student Book.

- You might also write the generalization on a sentence strip or poster to display for the duration of the lesson. Leave room for students to add some of their Prove It! words from Day 3.

- Students can preserve their word sorts by gluing the word cards to a separate sheet of paper. Otherwise, they can store their Sorting Boxes. (See page xi in this Teacher's Edition.)

Have students review the generalization and find more examples in available readable materials, such as picture books, storybooks, poems, or posters. Be sure students can read the words and that the words prove the generalization. You may want to adjust the number of words students should find, depending on students' needs. Invite students to share their lists with the class. Keep these lists in a class word bank or chart for future reference.

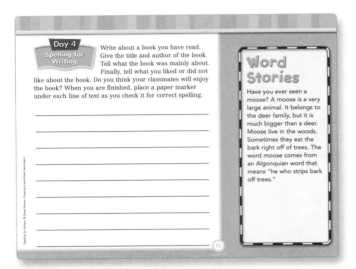

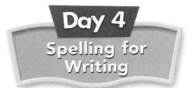

Have students use as many spelling words and Prove It! words in a book review. Students can write about a book they have read themselves or heard read aloud to them. The emphasis of this writing assignment is on using words that exhibit the word feature.

Offer these tips on writing a book review:

- Tell the name of the book and the author. Underline the title.

- Tell a little bit about the book—the names of the characters, the setting, what the book was mainly about.

- Tell what you liked or did not like about the book.

Proofreading Tip Review with students how to use a paper marker under a line of text so that the eyes can focus on just one line at a time. Ask students to tell why this is helpful.

Word Stories Have students describe a moose, if they can. If not, display a picture of one. Then explain that moose live all over North America. Native Americans knew them and knew their habits. They knew that moose often stripped bark right off of trees. Explain that the word *moose* comes from an Algonquian word for this animal. It means "he strips bark off trees." Discuss why this is an appropriate name. You may wish to remind students that *raccoon* and *skunk* are two other words from the Algonquian language.

Day 5
Word Play and Posttest

Ask students if they have ever done a word hunt before. If not, point out that spelling words are hidden among the letters. The spelling words are written across and down. The clues will help students know which way each word is written. Ask a volunteer to find the word that belongs with the first clue (*bark*). Make sure students know that they should write the word next to its clue. Have children work in pairs or groups to complete the puzzle. Afterwards, have them read their answers aloud.

Lesson 18
Posttest

Name _____

1. _____
2. _____
3. _____
4. _____
5. _____
6. _____
7. _____
8. _____

Day 5
Word Play

Some spelling words are hidden in this word-search puzzle. Look at each clue. Then hunt for the word in the puzzle. Circle the word when you find it. Then write it on the line next to the clue.

b	r	c	a	s	b	a	r	k
l	t	o	t	k	a	l	p	a
b	e	o	d	u	c	k	c	k
s	c	h	e	e	k	k	r	o
s	o	m	r	c	t	p	b	p
t	o	o	k	c	e	a	b	t
p	k	a	t	s	i	c	k	s
t	p	b	r	c	e	k	p	a

Across

tree part _____

water bird _____

face part _____

carried away _____

not well _____

Down

not front _____

heat up food _____

place in suitcase _____

Answers

Across

tree part (*bark*)

water bird (*duck*)

face part (*cheek*)

carried away (*took*)

not well (*sick*)

Down

not front (*back*)

heat up food (*cook*)

place in a suitcase (*pack*)

Posttest Have students tear out the perforated posttest. Students should pair up with their buddies or partners and exchange School Lists (page 69 in the Student Book). Students take turns testing each other on their respective spelling words. Collect the posttest sheets, score them, and record the correct response percentages (Teacher's Edition page 180). Mastery is 6 out of 8 words correct (75%). For students who do not achieve posttest mastery, see page xv in this Teacher's Edition.

Anchor Words After the posttest, have students select one or two anchor words to help them remember the word feature in this lesson. Record the words on the "Anchor Words" poster and refer to them in the Review lesson.

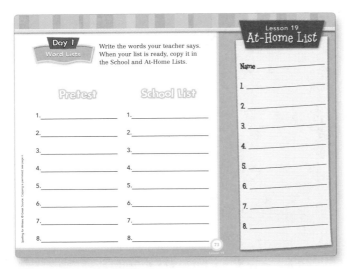

Lesson 19 — Plurals (-s). Add -s to change most singular nouns into plural nouns (*girls*).

Before Photocopy the Answer Key/Shopping List page (page 91 in this Teacher's Edition) for each student.

During Say each word in boldface, read the context sentence, and then repeat the word. Have students write the words in the Pretest column on page 73 of the Student Book.

After Distribute to students a copy of the Answer Key/Shopping List page so that they can correct their pretests.

- Students should cross out any misspelled words and write the correct spelling. Words that were correctly spelled can be replaced with words from the Shopping List. Assign the column from which students should choose their words. (See below.)

- Be sure that each student has a list of eight correctly spelled words, which they should copy into the School and At-Home Lists and the Sorting Boxes (page 91).

Pretest context sentences (spelling word in bold):

1. The **boy** who sits next to me is named Darren.
2. Two **boys** in this class live on my street.
3. One **girl** in my class was absent today.
4. Both of those **girls** play on my soccer team.
5. My best **friend** lives two blocks from me.
6. I invited six **friends** to my party.
7. This **school** was built five years ago.
8. I have attended two **schools** in this city.

At-Home List Send the At-Home List home so that families can help their students study the words and features. Several literacy activities are given on the back of the At-Home List: illustrating word pairs, arranging cut letters to spell words, and writing words using a simple number code.

> **NOTE** The Shopping List provides words below grade level (column 1), words at grade level (column 2), and more challenging words that have the feature (column 3).

Name _____

Shopping List

birds	apples	changes
rooms	planes	squares
trees	bases	coins
frogs	songs	colors

Sorting Boxes

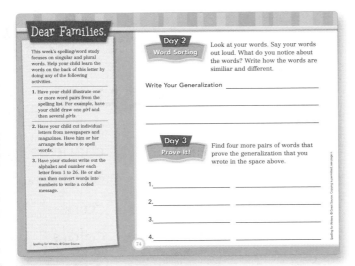

Have students look at the words carefully. Then have them decide for themselves a way or ways in which they can sort the words (do an open sort). Once they have made their sorts, ask them to say how the words are similar or different. What students say about the words shows you what they understand.

If students have not or cannot decide what the words have in common, model a way to sort all the words. You can use over-sized word cards (CD-ROM) or a cut-up transparency (Transparency 16) and overhead to facilitate your model. Use the following Think Aloud with your visuals.

> **TEACHER'S THINK ALOUD** I know I need to use my brain, ears, and eyes when I read these cards. All of my spelling words have something in common. So, I am going to think and look and listen. I notice that all my words mean one (*school*) or more than one (*schools*). The words that end in the letter *s* mean more than one.

- Have students sort the words from their own lists. Circulate around the classroom and have each group or pair describe their method of sorting.

- Bring the class together to reach a consensus about the generalization. An example is: *We can add an* s *to many words to make them plural.* Have students write their version on page 74 of the Student Book.

- You might also write the generalization on a sentence strip or poster to display for the duration of the lesson. Leave room for students to add some of their Prove It! words from Day 3.

- Students can preserve their word sorts by gluing the word cards to a separate sheet of paper. Otherwise, they can store their Sorting Boxes. (See page xi in this Teacher's Edition.)

Day 3
Prove It!

Have students review the generalization and find more examples in available readable materials, such as math books, counting books, and storybooks. Be sure students can read the words and that the words prove the generalization. You may want to adjust the number of words students should find, depending on students' needs. Invite students to share their lists with the class. Keep these lists in a class word bank or chart for future reference.

Day 4
Spelling for Writing

Have students write about themselves, using as many of the spelling words and Prove It! words as possible. Help students focus on just one part of their lives to write about, for example, life at home, life at school, their friends, and so forth.

Offer these tips for writing:

- Write about just one part of your life. Use the spelling words to help you choose.

- Try to think of details that will interest the reader.

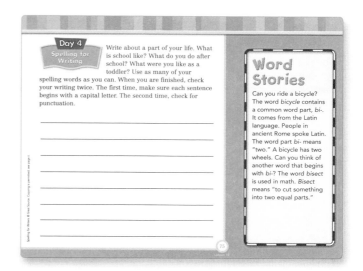

Proofreading Tip Teach students to look *for* something. Check for one thing at a time: mistakes that each student knows he or she makes consistently, punctuation at the end of each sentence, capital letters at the beginning of each sentence.

Word Stories Display a picture of a bicycle or have a volunteer describe one. Then write the word on the board, circling the word part *bi-*. Explain that this word part means "two." It appears in many words besides *bicycle*. Discuss the meaning of *bisect*. Then ask students if they have ever seen binoculars. Explain that this is another example of a word that contains *bi-*. You may also wish to point out that the word *cycle* comes from another ancient language—Greek. It means "circle." Ask a volunteer to tell which part of a bicycle forms a circle (wheels, gear hub).

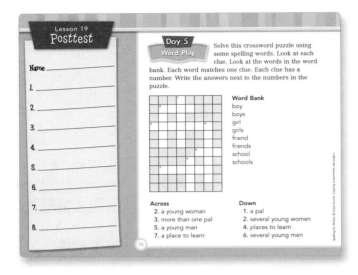

Show students the crossword puzzle and demonstrate how to match the clues with the puzzle. Ask a volunteer to find the word that belongs with the first clue (*girl*). Then ask another where she or he would write that word in the puzzle. Have students work in pairs or groups to complete the puzzle. Afterwards, have them read their answers aloud.

Answers

Across	**Down**
2. girl	1. friend
3. friends	2. girls
5. boy	4. schools
7. school	6. boys

Posttest Have students tear out the perforated posttest. Students should pair up with their buddies or partners and exchange School Lists (page 73 in the Student Book). Students take turns testing each other on their respective spelling words. Collect the posttest sheets, score them, and record the correct response percentages (Teacher's Edition page 180). Mastery is 6 out of 8 words correct (75%). For students who do not achieve posttest mastery, see page xv in this Teacher's Edition.

Anchor Words After the posttest, have students select one or two anchor words to help them remember the word feature in this lesson. Record the words on the "Anchor Words" poster and refer to them in the Review lesson.

Periodically, check writing samples from your students for transfer of the word features that have been taught. The features for the last three lessons are as follows:

Lesson 15: Consonant Blends
Lesson 18: Consonants (final *k*, *ck*)
Lesson 19: Plurals (-*s*)

Lesson 20

Plurals (-es). Add -es to change singular nouns that end with *s*, *sh*, *ch*, and *x* into plural nouns (*lunches*).

Day 1
Pretest and Word Lists

Before Photocopy the Answer Key/ Shopping List page (page 96 in this Teacher's Edition) for each student.

During Say each word in boldface, read the context sentence, and then repeat the word. Have students write the words in the Pretest column on page 77 of the Student Book.

After Distribute to students a copy of the Answer Key/Shopping List page so that they can correct their pretests.

- Students should cross out any misspelled words and write the correct spelling. Words that were correctly spelled can be replaced with words from the Shopping List. Assign a column from which students should choose their words. (See below.)

- Be sure that each student has a list of eight correctly spelled words, which they should copy into the School and At-Home Lists and the Sorting Boxes (page 96).

Pretest context sentences (spelling word in bold):

1. I am buying **lunch** today.
2. We all ate our **lunches** outside.
3. This book is an **inch** thick.
4. I have grown two **inches** since last year.
5. Do you want to wear a **dress** or pants?
6. All the girls wore white **dresses** for the event.
7. What's inside that **box** you're holding?
8. A pile of **boxes** is sitting in the hall.

At-Home List Send the At-Home List home so that families can help their students study the words and features. Several literacy activities are given on the back of the At-Home List: writing words using different colors for plurals, writing words crossword-puzzle style, finding plural words, and using toothpicks or magnetic letters to spell words.

> **NOTE** The Shopping List provides words below grade level (column 1), words at grade level (column 2), and more challenging words that have have the feature (column 3).

Name _____

Shopping List

bushes	classes	losses
kisses	flashes	guesses
dishes	taxes	riches
crashes	peaches	foxes

Sorting Boxes

Word Sorting

Have students look at the words carefully. Then have them decide for themselves a way or ways in which they can sort the words (do an open sort). Once they have made their sorts, ask them to say how the words are similar or different. What students say about the words shows you what they understand.

If students have not or cannot decide what the words have in common, model a way to sort all the words. You can use oversized word cards (CD-ROM) or a cut-up transparency (Transparency 17) and overhead to facilitate your model. Use the following Think Aloud with your visuals.

> **TEACHER'S THINK ALOUD** I notice that all my words mean one or more than one. I see the letters *es* at the end of the words to show more than one. I also see that the *es* comes after the letters *ch, sh, s,* or *x.* Those letters are at the end of the base word, which is the singular form of the word. The plural is formed by adding an *es* to the end of base words ending in these letters. I can hear the *es* sound to help me know how to spell these plural words.

- Have students sort the words from their own lists. Circulate around the classroom and have each group or pair describe their method of sorting.

- Then bring the class together to reach a consensus about the generalization. An example is this: *Words that end with* ch, sh, s, *or* x *need* -es *to form their plurals.* Have students write their version on page 78 of the Student Book.

- Point out that when students hear /ĕz/ at the end of a plural word, they should spell the word with *-es* at the end.

- You might also write the generalization on a sentence strip or poster to display for the duration of the lesson. Leave room for students to add some of their Prove It! words from Day 3.

- Students can preserve their word sorts by gluing the word cards to a separate sheet of paper. Otherwise, they can store their Sorting Boxes. (See page xi in this Teacher's Edition.)

Have students review the generalization and find more examples in available readable materials, such as math books, magazines, advertising fliers, and storybooks. Be sure students can read the words and that the words prove the generalization. You may want to adjust the number of words students should find, depending on students' needs. Invite students to share their lists with the class. Keep these lists in a class word bank or chart for future reference.

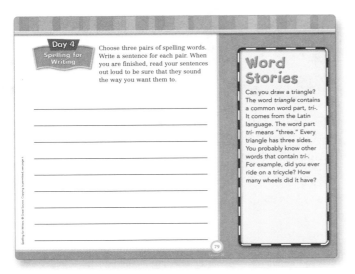

Students will choose three pairs of spelling words or Prove It! words and write a sentence for each word. Watch for the use of other plural words, too, so that you will know that students have internalized the generalizations about plurals.

Offer these tips for writing good sentences:

- Read them aloud to be sure that they read smoothly.

- Add or take away some words to make the sentences sound better.

- Begin each sentence with a capital letter and end each sentence with a period, a question mark, or an exclamation point.

Proofreading Tip Remind students that reading their writing out loud will help them hear any problems with it. They might notice that words were left out or that better words could be used. Reading out loud also slows the eyes down so that they can focus on each word more carefully.

Word Stories Draw a triangle on the board and write the word *triangle* next to it. Circle the word part *tri-*. Ask volunteers to count the number of angles and sides. Explain that *tri-* means "three," and it appears in many words besides *triangle*. Point out that the words *triplet*, *triple*, and *tripod* all contain *tri-*. Explain the meaning of each if students don't already know. Remind students that the word *bisect* means "to cut into two equal parts." Ask students to guess what *trisect* might mean ("to cut into three equal parts").

Day 5
Word Play and Posttest

Demonstrate how to count the syllables in words, using *bunch* and *bunches* as examples. Say each word aloud and ask how many vowel sounds students hear. Explain that they should write each syllable in its own box. Demonstrate this on the board. Draw two rectangles divided in half, similar to those on page 80 in the Student Book. In the first rectangle, write *bunch* in the first section and leave the second section blank. In the second rectangle, write *bunch* in one half and *es* in the other. Then write *ax* and *axes* on the board. Ask students how they would write these (*ax; ax, es*). Have children work in pairs or groups to complete the activity. Afterwards, have them read their answers aloud.

Posttest   Have students tear out the perforated posttest. Students should pair up with their buddies or partners and exchange School Lists (page 77 in the Student Book). Students take turns testing each other on their respective spelling words. Collect the posttest sheets, score them, and record the correct response percentages (Teacher's Edition page 180). Mastery is 6 out of 8 words correct (75%). For students who do not achieve posttest mastery, see page xv in this Teacher's Edition.

Anchor Words After the posttest, have students select one or two anchor words to help them remember the word feature in this lesson. Record the words on the "Anchor Words" poster and refer to them in the Review lesson.

Lesson 20
Posttest

Name _____

1. _____
2. _____
3. _____
4. _____
5. _____
6. _____
7. _____
8. _____

Day 5
Word Play

Write one syllable in each box. Some of your words have only one syllable. Some have two. You can tell a syllable because it has one vowel sound. Listen for each vowel sound. Use only the number of boxes that you need.

80

Lesson 21

Plurals (-s, -es). Add -s to form the plural of most words. Add -es to words that end with s, sh, ch, and x.

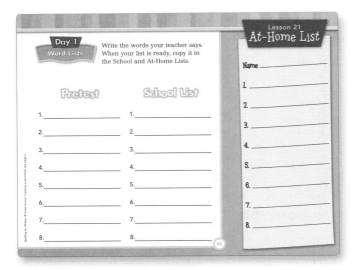

Before Photocopy the Answer Key/Shopping List page (page 101 in this Teacher's Edition) for each student.

During Say each word in boldface, read the context sentence, and then repeat the word. Have students write the words in the Pretest column on page 81 of the Student Book.

After Distribute to students a copy of the Answer Key/Shopping List page so that they can correct their pretests.

- Students should cross out any misspelled words and write the correct spelling. Words that were correctly spelled can be replaced with words from the Shopping List. Assign a column from which students should choose their words. (See below.)

- Be sure that each student has a list of eight correctly spelled words, which they should copy into the School and At-Home Lists and the Sorting Boxes (page 101).

Pretest context sentences (spelling word in bold):

1. Summer starts in five **days**.
2. The **bushes** outside my house stay green all year long.
3. Please put four **dishes** on the table.
4. I am acting in two different **plays** this year.
5. The **ashes** in the fireplace are still hot.
6. Are those birds **ducks** or geese?
7. Don't touch the ant **traps** that are in the kitchen.
8. People in fairy tales often get three **wishes**.

At-Home List Send the At-Home List home so that families can help their students study the words and features. Several literacy activities are given on the back of the At-Home List: finding plural words in newspapers and magazines, creating word-search puzzles, writing words using different colors for different letters, and drawing boxes of different shapes around the letters of spelling words.

NOTE The Shopping List provides words below grade level (column 1), words at grade level (column 2), and more challenging words that have the feature (column 3).

Name _____

Answer Key

1. days
2. bushes
3. dishes
4. plays
5. ashes
6. ducks
7. traps
8. wishes

Shopping List

games	blushes	houses
bags	branches	wagons
glasses	brothers	bathrooms
rashes	sisters	brushes

Sorting Boxes

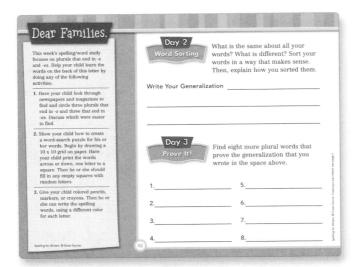

Have students look at the words carefully. Then have them decide for themselves a way or ways in which they can sort the words (do an open sort). Once they have made their sorts, ask them to say how the words are similar or different. What students say about the words shows you what they understand.

If students have not or cannot decide what the words have in common, model a way to sort all the words. You can use oversized word cards (CD-ROM) or a cut-up transparency (Transparency 18) and overhead to facilitate your model. Use the following Think Aloud with your visuals.

> **TEACHER'S THINK ALOUD** I know I need to use my brain, ears, and eyes when I read these cards. All of my spelling words have something in common. I notice that all my words are plural. Some of them end in *s* and some of them end in *es*. I already discovered that when the base word ends in *ch*, *sh*, *s*, or *x*, I spell the word with *es* to form the plural. Now I can see if that still works.

- Have students sort the words from their own lists. Circulate around the classroom and have each group or pair describe their method of sorting.

- Bring the class together to reach a consensus about the generalization. An example is this: *Add* -s *or* -es *to a single word to form a plural. How the base word ends tells me whether to add* -s *or* -es. Have students write their version on page 82 of the Student Book.

- Remind students that when they hear /ĕz/ at the end of a plural word, they should spell the word with *-es* at the end.

- You might also write the generalization on a sentence strip or poster to display for the duration of the lesson. Leave room for students to add some of their Prove It! words from Day 3.

- Students can preserve their word sorts by gluing the word cards to a separate sheet of paper. Otherwise, they can store their Sorting Boxes. (See page xi in this Teacher's Edition.)

Day 3
Prove It!

Have students review the generalization and find more examples in available readable materials, such as poetry books, storybooks, or textbooks. Be sure students can read the words and that the words prove the generalization. You may want to adjust the number of words students should find, depending on students' needs. Invite students to share their lists with the class. Keep these lists in a class word bank or chart for future reference.

Day 4
Spelling for Writing

Have students write a description of an outdoor scene. Discuss some ideas that students can choose from. Explain that a description should help the reader see the scene, so the writers should use sensory details that tell what the reader should see, hear, touch, or smell. (Taste probably will not apply.) Encourage students to use as many spelling words and Prove It! words as they can. However, watch for the use of other plural words, too, so that you will know that students have internalized the generalizations about plural words.

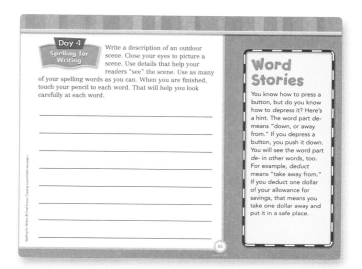

Offer these tips for writing a description:

- Close your eyes to picture the scene or draw a picture before writing.

- Make a list of sensory details.

- Choose an order in which to list the details; for example, left to right, top to bottom, or by importance (most important detail first or last).

Proofreading Tip Remind students that proofreading must be done slowly and carefully. Demonstrate for the students how to touch every word with a finger or pencil so that their eyes concentrate on one word at a time.

Word Stories Write the words *press* and *depress* on the board. Ask how they are alike and different. Discuss the meaning of the word *press.* Then point out that the word part *de-* gives a clue to the meaning of *depress,* because it means "down or away from." Provide students with additional examples, such as *decrease* (to drop in number or size), and *decline* (fall to a lower level). You may wish to point out that *de-* can have other meanings as well. For example, in *defrost,* it means "to remove."

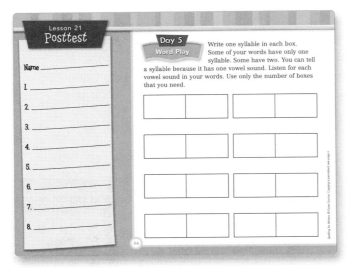

Demonstrate how to count the syllables in words, using *wings* and *beaches* as examples. Say each word aloud and ask how many vowel sounds students hear. Explain that they should write each syllable in its own box. Demonstrate this on the board. Draw a rectangle divided in half, similar to the ones on page 84 in the Student Book. Write *wings* in one half and leave the other half blank. Then write *beaches* on the board. Ask students how they would write this in a box (*beach, es*). Afterwards, have them read their answers aloud.

Posttest   Have students tear out the perforated posttest. Students should pair up with their buddies or partners and exchange School Lists (page 81 in the Student Book). Students take turns testing each other on their respective spelling words. Collect the posttest sheets, score them, and record the correct response percentages (Teacher's Edition page 180). Mastery is 6 out of 8 words correct (75%). For students who do not achieve posttest mastery, see page xv in this Teacher's Edition.

Anchor Words After the posttest, have students select one or two anchor words to help them remember the word feature in this lesson. Record the words on the "Anchor Words" poster and refer to them in the Review lesson.

Lesson 22 Plurals (*y* to *i*, irregular forms). When some words are changed to plurals, their spelling changes (cries, children).

Day 1
Pretest and Word Lists

Before Photocopy the Answer Key/ Shopping List page (page 106 in this Teacher's Edition) for each student.

During Say each word in boldface, read the context sentence, and then repeat the word. Have students write the words in the Pretest column on page 85 of the Student Book.

After Distribute to students a copy of the Answer Key/Shopping List page so that they can correct their pretests.

- Students should cross out any misspelled words and write the correct spelling. Words that were correctly spelled can be replaced with words from the Shopping List. Assign a column from which students should choose their words. (See below.)

- Be sure that each student has a list of eight correctly spelled words, which they should copy into the School and At-Home Lists and the Sorting Boxes (page 106).

Pretest context sentences (spelling word in bold):

1. Did you hear a **cry** for help?
2. Their many **cries** for help were answered.
3. The **sky** is bright blue today.
4. I hope we have blue **skies** for our picnic.
5. That **child** is waiting for the bus to come.
6. Several other **children** get off at my bus stop.
7. Is that **man** your father?
8. Two **men** lifted the desk and moved it into the next room.

At-Home List Send the At-Home List home so that families can help their students study the words and features. Several literacy activities are given on the back of the At-Home List: playing "Memory" with word pairs, listing words in alphabetical order, saying the singular and plural forms of words from a favorite book, and using letters cut from print media to spell words.

> **NOTE** The Shopping List provides words below grade level (column 1), words at grade level (column 2), and more challenging words that have the feature (column 3).

Name _____

Answer Key

1. cry
2. cries
3. sky
4. skies
5. child
6. children
7. man
8. men

Shopping List

flies	copies	candies
tries	ladies	countries
cities	feet	moose
babies	mice	deer

Sorting Boxes

Have students look at the words carefully. Then have them decide for themselves a way or ways in which they can sort the words (do an open sort). Once they have made their sorts, ask them to say how the words are similar or different. What students say about the words shows you what they understand.

If students have not or cannot decide what the words have in common, model a way to sort all the words. You can use oversized word cards (CD-ROM) or a cut-up transparency (Transparency 19) and overhead to facilitate your model. Use the following Think Aloud with your visuals.

TEACHER'S THINK ALOUD When I look at my words, I notice that some of them mean one and some are plural. I'm going to sort my words into two groups; the words that mean one and the words that are mean more than one. When I look at the words in my plural group, I notice that in some of the words the vowel letter *y* has been changed to *i* before adding *es*. Some of the other plural words are spelled differently or exactly the same but no *s* or *es* has been added.

- Have students sort the words from their own lists. Circulate around the classroom and have each group or pair describe their method of sorting.

- Then bring the class together to reach a consensus about the generalization. Example: *When a base word ends with a consonant and then* y, *I change the* y *to* i *and add* es. *Other times I need to spell special words that are not spelled with an* s *or an* es *at the end to mean plural.* Have students write their version on page 86 of the Student Book.

- Explain that there are other ways to make plurals without adding -*s* or -*es*; for example, sometimes the spelling doesn't change (*deer*), sometimes the vowel changes (*men*), or letters are added (*children*).

- You might also write the generalization on a sentence strip or poster to display for the duration of the lesson. Leave room for students to add some of their Prove It! words from Day 3.

- Students can preserve their word sorts by gluing the word cards to a separate sheet of paper. Otherwise, they can store their Sorting Boxes. (See page xi in this Teacher's Edition.)

Have students review the generalization and find more examples in available readable materials, such as storybooks, nonfiction books, or magazines. Be sure students can read the words, and that the words prove the generalization. You may want to adjust the number of words students should find, depending on students' needs. Invite students to share their lists with the class. Keep these lists in a class word bank or chart for future reference.

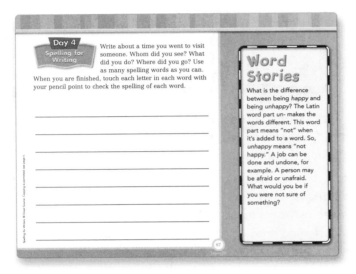

Students will write a personal narrative about a time they went to visit someone. Have students describe their ideas and make a list of possible writing topics from which students can choose. Encourage students to use as many spelling words and Prove It! words as they can. However, watch for the use of other plural words, too, so that you will know that students have internalized the generalizations about plural words.

Offer these tips for writing a personal narrative:

• A narrative tells about a personal experience in the order in which things happened.

• Focus on an interesting part of the visit, rather than just listing the events.

• Grab the reader's attention with the first sentence.

Proofreading Tip Using a large copy of a text, remind students how to touch every letter with a pencil to make sure that all the letters are correct and none were left out.

Word Stories Write the words *tie* and *untie* on the board. Ask how they are alike and different. Discuss the meaning of the word *tie*. Then point out that the word part *un-* changes the meaning of a word, because *un-* means "not" or "the opposite of." Provide students with additional examples, such as *button/unbutton*, *lucky/unlucky*, and *safe/unsafe*. Then ask students what the opposite of the following words might be: *painted* (*unpainted*), *hurt* (*unhurt*), *true* (*untrue*), and *spoken* (*unspoken*).

Day 5
Word Play and Posttest

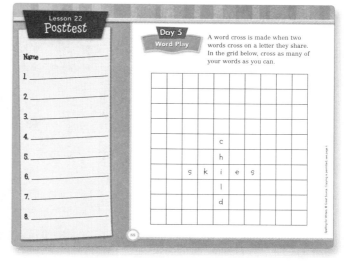

Day 5
Word Play

A word cross is made when two words cross on a letter they share. In the grid below, cross as many of your words as you can.

Students will fill in the grid on Student Book page 88 by crossing their words on the common letters. An example is shown. Once students have crossed as many words of their own as they can, suggest that students swap books and add some of their words to a buddy's word-cross grid.

Posttest Have students tear out the perforated posttest. Students should pair up with their buddies or partners and exchange School Lists (page 85 in the Student Book). Students take turns testing each other on their respective spelling words. Collect the posttest sheets, score them, and record the correct response percentages (Teacher's Edition page 180). Mastery is 6 out of 8 words correct (75%). For students who do not achieve posttest mastery, see page xv in this Teacher's Edition.

Anchor Words After the posttest, have students select one or two anchor words to help them remember the word feature in this lesson. Record the words on the "Anchor Words" poster and refer to them in the Review lesson.

Periodically, check writing samples from your students for transfer of the word features that have been taught. The features for the last three lessons are as follows:

Lesson 20: Plurals (-*es*)
Lesson 21: Plurals (-*s, -es*)
Lesson 22: Plurals (*y to i, irregular form*s)

Lesson 23 Consonants (*silent letter patterns*). Consonant letters can make a pattern in which one is silent, as in *knew* and *wrap*.

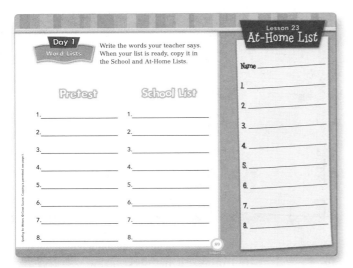

Day 1
Pretest and Word Lists

Before Photocopy the Answer Key/ Shopping List page (page 111 in this Teacher's Edition) for each student.

During Say each word in boldface, read the context sentence, and then repeat the word. Have students write the words in the Pretest column on page 89 of the Student Book.

After Distribute to students a copy of the Answer Key/Shopping List page so that they can correct their pretests.

- Students should cross out any misspelled words and write the correct spelling. Words that were correctly spelled can be replaced with words from the Shopping List. Assign a column from which students should choose their words. (See below.)

- Be sure that each student has a list of eight correctly spelled words, which they should copy into the School and At-Home Lists and the Sorting Boxes (page 111).

Pretest context sentences (spelling word in bold):

1. I **knew** the answer to every math question yesterday.
2. Please **write** your name on the paper.
3. This **knot** keeps coming untied.
4. I **wrote** a silly poem yesterday.
5. I need paper so I can **wrap** this gift.
6. Yes, I **know** how to tie a shoe.
7. When did you scrape your **knee**?
8. That old car we passed was a **wreck**.

At-Home List Send the At-Home List home so that families can help their students study the words and features. Several literacy activities are given on the back of the At-Home List: conducting a word hunt, writing rhyming words, writing silent letters in a different color, and writing word pyramids for spelling words.

> **NOTE** The Shopping List provides words below grade level (column 1), words at grade level (column 2), and more challenging words that have the feature (column 3).

Name _____

Answer Key

1. knew	**5.** wrap
2. write	**6.** know
3. knot	**7.** knee
4. wrote	**8.** wreck

Shopping List

knit	kneel	knapsack
knife	knead	knuckle
wring	wreath	wrinkle
wrong	wrist	wrestle

Sorting Boxes

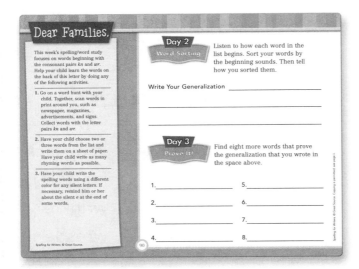

Day 2
Word Sorting

Have students look at the words carefully. Then have them decide for themselves a way or ways in which they can sort the words (do an open sort). Once they have made their sorts, ask them to say how the words are similar or different. What students say about the words shows you what they understand.

If students have not or cannot decide what the words have in common, model a way to sort all the words. You can use over-sized word cards (CD-ROM) or a cut-up transparency (Transparency 20) and overhead to facilitate your model. Use the following Think Aloud with your visuals.

> **TEACHER'S THINK ALOUD** First, I will look at all my words. Then, I will read them out loud. I see that all my words have a consonant at the beginning. The pairs in common are *kn* and *wr*. So, my eye sees a consonant pair, but my ear hears only the second consonant in each pair. So, in the word *knee*, the first consonant (*k*) is silent. In the word *wrap*, the *w* is silent. So, I need to really look carefully at my words when I spell them because my ear does not hear the first consonant.

- Have students sort the words from their own lists. Circulate around the classroom and have each group or pair describe their method of sorting.

- Bring the class together to reach a consensus about the generalization. An example is this: *In some consonant pairs, the first consonant is silent. Two of those pairs are* kn *and* wr. Have students write their version on page 90 of the Student Book.

- You might also write the generalization on a sentence strip or poster to display for the duration of the lesson. Leave room for students to add some of their Prove It! words from Day 3.

- Students can preserve their word sorts by gluing the word cards to a separate sheet of paper. Otherwise, they can store their Sorting Boxes. (See page xi in this Teacher's Edition.)

Day 3

Prove It!

Have students review the generalization and find more examples in available readable materials, such as storybooks, activity or craft books, or workbooks. Be sure students can read the words and that the words prove the generalization. You may want to adjust the number of words students should find, depending on students' needs. Invite students to share their lists with the class. Keep these lists in a class word bank or chart for future reference.

Day 4

Spelling for Writing

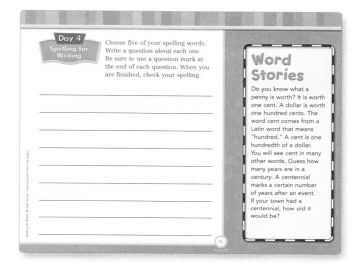

Students will choose five of their spelling words or Prove It! words and write a question about each word. When students have finished writing and proofreading their questions, ask for volunteers to read their sentences aloud. Model how to use your voice to indicate a question.

Offer these tips for writing good sentences:

- Read them aloud to be sure that they read smoothly.

- Add or take away some words to make the sentences sound better.

- Begin each sentence with a capital letter and place a question mark at the end of each question.

Proofreading Tip Remind students once again that proofreading should be done slowly and carefully. Review how to use a piece of paper as a marker under each line so the eyes concentrate on one line at a time.

Word Stories Display a penny and ask students what it is. Ask how much it is worth. Write the word *cent* on the board and explain that it comes from a Latin word that means "one hundred." Discuss how many pennies are in a dollar, how many years are in a century, and how many years would pass before a town had a centennial. Then ask students if they have ever seen a centigrade thermometer. Explain or remind students that it uses a scale (known as the Celsius scale) that is divided into 100 degrees. On a centigrade thermometer, the freezing point for water is 0 degrees and the boiling point is 100 degrees. *Centigrade* comes from *cent* plus the Latin word *gradus*, which means "step" or "degree."

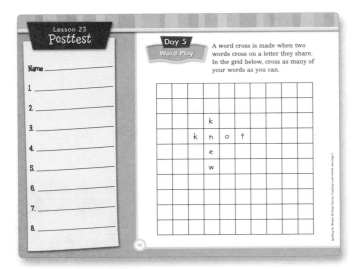

Students will fill in the grid on Student Book page 92 by crossing their words on the common letters. An example is shown. Once students have crossed as many words of their own as they can, suggest that students swap books and add some of their words to a buddy's word-cross grid.

Posttest   Have students tear out the perforated posttest. Students should pair up with their buddies or partners and exchange School Lists (page 89 in the Student Book). Students take turns testing each other on their respective spelling words. Collect the posttest sheets, score them, and record the correct response percentages (Teacher's Edition page 180). Mastery is 6 out of 8 words correct (75%). For students who do not achieve posttest mastery, see page xv in this Teacher's Edition.

Anchor Words After the posttest, have students select one or two anchor words to help them remember the word feature in this lesson. Record the words on the "Anchor Words" poster and refer to them in the Review lesson.

Lesson 24

Long Vowels (*silent letter patterns*). Sometimes vowel letters make a pattern in which the vowel is long and one or more other letters are silent (*night, yellow*).

Day 1
Pretest and Word Lists

Before Photocopy the Answer Key/ Shopping List page (page 116 in this Teacher's Edition) for each student.

During Say each word in boldface, read the context sentence, and then repeat the word. Have students write the words in the Pretest column on page 93 of the Student Book.

After Distribute to students a copy of the Answer Key/Shopping List page so that they can correct their pretests.

- Students should cross out any misspelled words and write the correct spelling. Words that were correctly spelled can be replaced with words from the Shopping List. Assign a column from which students should choose their words. (See below.)

- Be sure that each student has a list of eight correctly spelled words, which they should copy into the School and At-Home Lists and the Sorting Boxes (page 116).

Pretest context sentences (spelling word in bold):

1. Most people sleep at **night**.
2. That shelf is too **high** for me to reach.
3. My favorite color is **yellow**.
4. We get very little **snow** in this area.
5. The fence is **low**, so I can see over it.
6. My seat is in the back **row** of desks.
7. Do we turn left or **right**?
8. Your garden is a beautiful **sight**!

At-Home List Send the At-Home List home so that families can help their students study the words and features. Several literacy activities are given on the back of the At-Home List: making scrambled word puzzles, drawing pictures that contain hidden words, outlining words in color, and using a finger to write words in a person's open palm.

> **NOTE** The Shopping List provides words below grade level (column 1), words at grade level (column 2), and more challenging words that have the feature (column 3).

Name _____

Shopping List

light   bright   sigh

might   fight   thigh

bow   crow   show

blow   grow   below

Sorting Boxes

Day 2
Word Sorting

Have students look at the words carefully. Then have them decide for themselves a way or ways in which they can sort the words (do an open sort). Once they have made their sorts, ask them to say how the words are similar or different. What students say about the words shows you what they understand.

If students have not or cannot decide what the words have in common, model a way to sort all the words. You can use oversized word cards (CD-ROM) or a cut-up transparency (Transparency 21) and overhead to facilitate your model. Use the following Think Aloud with your visuals.

Dear Families,

This week's spelling/word study focuses on words that contain the vowel patterns *igh* (as in *flight*) and *ow* (as in *slow*). Help your child learn the words on the back of this letter by doing any of the following activities.

1. Help your child make scrambled word puzzles for you to solve. Show him or her how to scramble the letters of each word and list the scrambled words in one column. Next to each word, have your child draw a line to write on. See how many of the words you can unscramble and write on the lines.

2. Have your child draw a picture and try to hide a spelling word somewhere in it.

3. Have your child write a word and then trace its outline in another color. He or she may wish to draw additional outlines in different colors around the first.

Spelling for Writers © Great Source.

Day 2 Word Sorting — Listen to the vowel sound in each word. Sort your words by the way the vowels sound. Then tell how you sorted them.

Write Your Generalization _____

Day 3 Prove It! — Find eight more words that prove the generalization that you wrote in the space above.

1. _____ 5. _____
2. _____ 6. _____
3. _____ 7. _____
4. _____ 8. _____

TEACHER'S THINK ALOUD When I read my words aloud, I notice that all my words have a long vowel sound. I hear the long sound of *i* and the long sound of *o*. My eye sees that the words in the long *i* category are all spelled *igh*. The *gh* is silent, my ear only hears the long *i*. I see that the words in the long *o* category are all spelled *ow*. The *w* is silent, my ear only hears the long *o*. I can sort my words into two categories.

- Have students sort the words from their own lists. Circulate around the classroom and have each group or pair describe their method of sorting.

- Then bring the class together to reach a consensus about the generalization. Example: *One way to spell long* i *is* igh, *and one way to spell long* o *is* ow. Have students write their version on page 94 of the Student Book.

- Remind students that when they spell a word that has a long vowel sound, they will have to remember that they probably need more than one letter to represent the vowel sound.

- You might also write the generalization on a sentence strip or poster to display for the duration of the lesson. Leave room for students to add some of their Prove It! words from Day 3.

- Students can preserve their word sorts by gluing the word cards to a separate sheet of paper. Otherwise, they can store their Sorting Boxes. (See page xi in this Teacher's Edition.)

Have students review the generalization and find more examples in available readable materials, such as poems, storybooks, textbooks, or trade books. Be sure students can read the words and that the words prove the generalization. You may want to adjust the number of words students should find, depending on students' needs. Invite students to share their lists with the class. Keep these lists in a class word bank or chart for future reference.

NOTE Students might find *ow* words that have the long *o* sound; for example, *snow*. Put these words in a separate category.

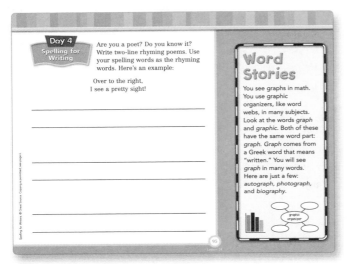

Have students write couplets, using as many of their spelling words or Prove It! words as they can. A couplet consists of two-lines that rhyme at the end. For example:

Over to the right,
I see a pretty sight!

Review the concept of rhyme with students before they begin to write. Have them suggest word pairs that rhyme. Have students write as many couplets as they can manage.

Proofreading Tip Teach students to look *for* something. Check for one thing at a time: mistakes that each student knows he or she makes consistently, punctuation at the end of each sentence, capital letters at the beginning of each sentence.

Word Stories Tell students that many word in English have word parts that come from other languages. The word part *graph* is a good example. It means "written" and comes from the Greek language. Write the words *graph* and *graphic* on the board. Then show students an example of a graph, perhaps from a math book, and of a graphic organizer, such as a Venn diagram. Explain that both of these contain written information. Discuss the words *autograph* (written signature), *photograph* (image that is "written" on paper), and *graph paper*. Help students understand the meanings of any terms that are unfamiliar.

Day 5
Word Play and Posttest

Tell students that they are going to play a new game. Students will first unscramble words and write them correctly. After students have unscrambled the words, they should look for letters that have numerals below them. These letters should be written in the blanks at the bottom of the page. Make sure students realize that the letters should be written above the corresponding numbers. Demonstrate how to match them. Explain to students that after they fill in all the blanks, they will have the answer to the riddle at the bottom of the page. Work with students to complete the first word. Then have them work independently or in pairs to complete the activity. Afterwards, have them read their answers aloud.

Answers

1. yellow	5. low
2. night	6. snow
3. row	7. right
4. sight	8. high

Riddle: Climb a tree and act like a nut!

Posttest Have students tear out the perforated posttest. Students should pair up with their buddies or partners and exchange School Lists (page 93 in the Student Book). Students take turns testing each other on their respective spelling words. Collect the posttest sheets, score them, and record the correct response percentages (Teacher's Edition page 180). Mastery is 6 out of 8 words correct (75%). For students who do not achieve posttest mastery, see page xv in this Teacher's Edition.

Anchor Words After the posttest, have students select one or two anchor words to help them remember the word feature in this lesson. Record the words on the "Anchor Words" poster and refer to them in the Review lesson.

Lesson 25 Long Vowels (*silent letter patterns*). Sometimes vowel letters make a pattern in which one vowel is long and one is silent, as in *sail* and *reach*.

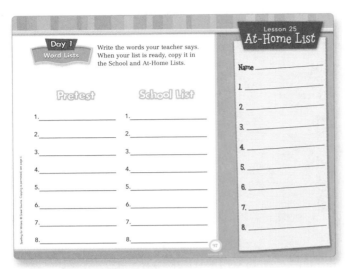

Before Photocopy the Answer Key/Shopping List page (page 121 in this Teacher's Edition) for each student.

During Say each word in boldface, read the context sentence, and then repeat the word. Have students write the words on page 97 of the Student Book.

After Distribute to students a copy of the Answer Key/Shopping List page so that they can correct their pretests.

- Students should cross out any misspelled words and write the correct spelling. Words that were correctly spelled can be replaced with words from the Shopping List. Assign a column from which students should choose their words. (See below.)

- Be sure that each student has a list of eight correctly spelled words, which they should copy into the School and At-Home Lists and the Sorting Boxes (page 121).

Pretest context sentences (spelling word in bold):

1. I would like to **sail** to a tropical island.
2. Can you **reach** the top shelf?
3. We can walk on a **trail** through the woods.
4. I have a great **deal** of work to do.
5. Please **mail** this letter for me.
6. The **sea** looks very blue and calm.
7. I already **paid** for lunch.
8. The restaurant serves both coffee and **tea**.

At-Home List Send the At-Home List home so that families can help their students study the words and features. Several literacy activities are given on the back of the At-Home List: having a word hunt, writing words that rhyme with list words, writing words crossword-puzzle style, and circling words written in a word chain.

> **NOTE** The Shopping List provides words below grade level (column 1), words at grade level (column 2), and more challenging words that have the feature (column 3).

Name _____

Answer Key

1. sail	**5.** mail
2. reach	**6.** sea
3. trail	**7.** paid
4. deal	**8.** tea

Shopping List

rain	main	raise
wait	pain	sailboat
easy	clean	jeans
pea	leaf	leap

Sorting Boxes

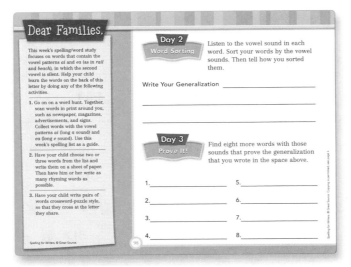

Have students look at the words carefully. Then have them decide for themselves a way or ways in which they can sort the words (do an open sort). Once they have made their sorts, ask them to say how the words are similar or different. What students say about the words shows you what they understand.

If students have not or cannot decide what the words have in common, model a way to sort all the words. You can use over-sized word cards (CD-ROM) or a cut-up transparency (Transparency 22) and overhead to facilitate your model. Use the following Think Aloud with your visuals.

> **TEACHER'S THINK ALOUD** I know I need to use my brain, ears, and eyes when I read these cards. All of my spelling words have something in common. So, I am going to think and look and listen. I notice that all my words have long vowel sounds — long *a* or long *e*. My eye sees that in the long *a* category, the words are spelled *ai*. I hear the *a*, and my eye sees the *i*, but it is silent. My eye sees that in the long *e* category, the words are spelled *ea*. I hear the *e*, and my eye sees the *a*, but it is silent.

- Have students sort the words from their own lists. Circulate around the classroom and have each group or pair describe their method of sorting.

- Bring the class together to reach a consensus about the generalization. Example: *One way to spell long* a *is* ai, *and one way to spell long* e *is* ea. Have students write their version on page 98 of the Student Book.

- You might also write the generalization on a sentence strip or poster to display for the duration of the lesson. Leave room for students to add some of their Prove It! words from Day 3.

- Students can preserve their word sorts by gluing the word cards to a separate sheet of paper. Otherwise, they can store their Sorting Boxes. (See page xi in this Teacher's Edition.)

Day 3
Prove It!

Have students review the generalization and find more examples in available readable materials, such as storybooks, rhyming books, or labeled picture books. Be sure students can read the words, and that the words prove the generalization. You may want to adjust the number of words students should find, depending on students' needs. Invite students to share their lists with the class. Keep these lists in a class word bank or chart for future reference.

NOTE Students might find *ea* words that have the short e sound; for example, *head*. Put these words in a separate category.

Day 4
Spelling for Writing

Have students choose four of their spelling words or Prove It! words and write a riddle for each one. The spelling words will be the answers to the riddles. Review with students what a riddle is and what it does. Use this example:

What is a hot drink that is not coffee?
(*tea*)

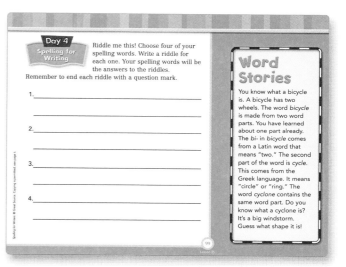

Students should write the answer at the end of each riddle, Then, have them work with spelling buddies to answer each others' riddles.

Proofreading Tip The riddles will be read aloud, so all the words must be correct. Instruct the students to read the riddles aloud to make sure that no words were left out.

Word Stories Tell students that many words in English have word parts that come from other languages. Remind students that they learned about the word part *bi-* in an earlier lesson. Briefly review its meaning ("two"). The word part *cycle* is another useful word part. It means "circle or ring" and comes from the Greek language. Ask students what parts of a bicycle form a circle (the wheels). Then explain that a tornado is a type of *cyclone*. If possible, display a picture, perhaps from a dictionary or science book. Point out that the winds in such storms form circles. Discuss the meaning of the word *cycle*, which students have seen in science when they studied the water cycle. Remind them that a *cycle* is a series of events that repeats itself. Have students explain what the circle or ring is in a cycle.

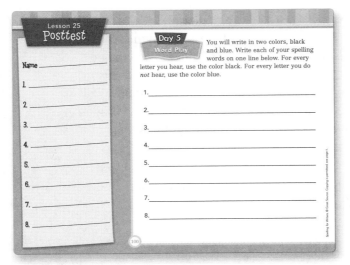

Distribute colored pens, crayons, or markers. Make sure each student has a black and a blue one. Explain that they will write their list words using one color for silent letters and another color for letters that they hear. Demonstrate this with the word *read.* Using large letters on a piece of paper, write the *r, e,* and *d* in black and the *a* in blue. Then work with students to do another word together before having them complete the activity independently.

Posttest Have students tear out the perforated posttest. Students should pair up with their buddies or partners and exchange School Lists (page 97 in the Student Book). Students take turns testing each other on their respective spelling words. Collect the posttest sheets, score them, and record the correct response percentages (Teacher's Edition page 180). Mastery is 6 out of 8 words correct (75%). For students who do not achieve posttest mastery, see page xv in this Teacher's Edition.

Anchor Words After the posttest, have students select one or two anchor words to help them remember the word feature in this lesson. Record the words on the "Anchor Words" poster and refer to them in the Review lesson.

Periodically, check writing samples from your students for transfer of the word features that have been taught. The features for the last three lessons are as follows:

Lesson 23: Consonants (*silent letter patterns*)
Lesson 24: Long Vowels (*silent letter patterns*)
Lesson 25: Long Vowels (*silent letter patterns*)

Lesson 26 Review (Lessons 18-25).

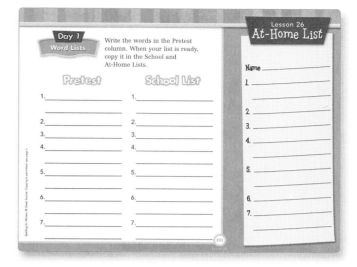

Day 1
Pretest and Word Lists

Before There are three options for selecting the pretest words. Choose the one most appropriate for your students.

1. Have students think of words that fit the spelling patterns and write them.

2. Use the words that you and your class collected on the "Anchor Words" poster.

3. Use the examples given on page 126.

If you will dictate the words, either from the "Anchor Words" poster or from page 126, make an answer key by writing the words on a copy of Copy Master 1. Photocopy the filled-in answer key page for each student.

During Announce each word feature as listed on page 126. As you say each feature, also state the generalization and give the words or ask students to think of words. Students will write one or two words for each feature on page 101 of the Student Book.

After If you dictated words, distribute a copy of the answer key so that students can self-correct their pretests. Otherwise, correct students' pretests.

• For any word that students got correct, send them back to the lesson for that feature to select a word from their Prove It! List they want to learn to spell.

• Be sure that each student has a list of correctly spelled words, which they should copy into the School and At-Home Lists and the Sorting Boxes (use Copy Master 1 for the Sorting Boxes).

At-Home List Have students tear out the perforated At-Home List and take it home to use with families. Several literacy activities are given on the back of the At-Home List: having a word hunt, finding plurals and identifying the singular form, and forming words by changing initial or final letters.

Word Features and Generalizations

1. **Consonants (final _k, ck_).** At the end of a word, the /k/ sound can be represented by _k_ or _ck_, as in _took_ and _back_. (_Lesson 18_)

2. **Plurals _(-s)_.** Add _–s_ to change most singular nouns into plural nouns (_girls_). (_Lesson 19_)

3. **Plurals _(-es)_.** Add _–es_ to change singular nouns that end with _s, sh, ch_, and _x_ into plural nouns (_lunches_). (_Lessons 20, 21_)

4. **Plurals (_y_ to _i_, irregular forms).** When some words are changed to plurals, their spelling changes (_cries, children_). (_Lesson 22_)

5. **Consonants (silent letter patterns).** Consonant letters can make a pattern in which one is silent, as in _knew_ and _wrap_. (_Lesson 23_)

6. **Long Vowels (silent letter patterns).** Sometimes letters make a pattern in which the vowel is long and one or more letters are silent, as in _night_ and _yellow_. (_Lesson 24_)

7. **Long Vowels (silent letter patterns).** Sometimes vowel letters make a pattern in which one vowel is long and one is silent, as in _sail_ and _reach_. (_Lesson 25_)

Day 2
Word Sorting

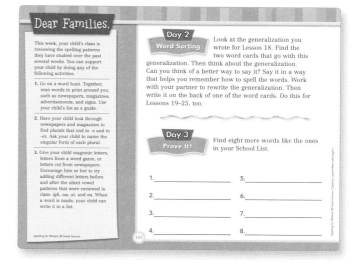

Today students will revisit the generalizations they wrote for Lessons 18–25. They will read them and then decide if they could be stated more clearly.

- Have students cut apart the Sorting Boxes to create word cards for this activity (Copy Master).

- Have them form pairs and turn to page 70 of their Student Books.

- Both students should read the generalization they wrote for Lesson 18 and identify the word cards that relate to this generalization. Then they should ask themselves if the generalization is clear. Could it be stated in a way that would be more helpful in remembering how to spell the words?

- You might work through the first generalization with the class to show students how to clarify and improve the wording.

- Students should then write the best version of the generalization on the back of a relevant word card and move on to the next generalization (Lesson 19).

As a closing step, have students work in pairs to sort their words into groups that make sense. Circulate through the room to talk with students about their word sorts. Students' explanations of their sorts tell you what they understand about how words work.

After students revisit and revise several general-izations for this lesson's review, send them off to find in readable materials more examples that prove as many of the generalizations as possible to be true. Provide appropriate reading materials, such as storybooks, poetry books, newspapers, and textbooks. Be sure that students can read the words they find and that their words prove each generalization. Adjust the amount and kind of reading material students will use as well as the number of words they should find, according to their needs. You might want to limit the scope of the word hunt by having some students search for words that prove only one or two of the generalizations.

Day 3
Prove It!

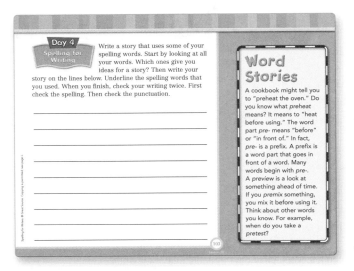

Day 4
Spelling for Writing

Although students should write about their stories independently, encourage them to work with partners to brain-storm story ideas. One way to begin is by trying to pair nouns and verbs, which may then suggest ideas for characters or situations. For example, the words *friends* and *mail* might suggest a story about a friend who moves away.

Offer these tips to students as they plan their stories:

- Write about just one event.

- Make sure the story has a clear beginning, middle, and end.

- Show the reader what the setting is like, don't just tell. ("Cars whooshed by and angry horns honked" is better than "A lot of traffic went by.")

Proofreading Tip Remind students that a good proofreader checks a piece of writing for only one thing at a time. For example, check the spelling the first time through and check the punctuation on the second pass.

Word Stories Tell students that many words in English have word parts from other languages. Remind students that they learned about the word part *re-* in an earlier lesson. Briefly review its meaning ("again"). Then point out that *pre-* is another useful word part. Write *premix* on the board. Ask a volunteer to draw a line between the prefix and the root word. Discuss its meaning and then write *pretest* on the board. Ask a volunteer to name the root word. Then have students tell when they take pretests (before the real tests).

Lesson 26
Posttest

Name _____

1. _____
2. _____
3. _____
4. _____
5. _____
6. _____
7. _____

Day 5
Word Play

Today you will play "Look Sharp"! Look at each set of words. Say them aloud to yourself. Listen to them. Three of the words in each set are alike in some way. One word is not like the rest. Cross out that word. Then write another word that belongs in the set.

1. book, peek, check, look _____
2. boys, star, schools, songs _____
3. kisses, wishes, tops, foxes _____
4. men, women, child, feet _____
5. not, knee, knit, know _____
6. sigh, right, pig, light _____
7. snow, now, low, throw _____
8. deal, sea, read, sail _____

104

Tell students that they will play a game that requires them to look, read, and think. Review the directions on page 104 of the Student Book and make sure students understand that each set of words contains one that does not belong. Explain that the reason a word might not belong will change from group to group. Students need to look at all the words in a group, read them, and think about how most are alike. Then they should cross out the word that does not belong and come up with a new word that would belong. You may wish to work through the first item with students. Discuss why *check* does not belong with the others (the other words all end with just *k*). Then ask volunteers to suggest words that would belong in the group (e.g., *cook, speak*). After they have completed the activity, have them compare their answers with those of partners. (**Answers: 1.** check, **2.** star, **3.** tops, **4.** child, **5.** not, **6.** pig, **7.** now, **8.** sail)

Review Activities Other activities that students can do to review the words include the following:

- Have students choose a set of Sorting Boxes from a previous lesson and time themselves when they sort the cards. Students should sort them several times to see whether their sorting time gets faster. (Copy Masters of the pretest words can be found in the Transparencies and Copy Masters folder. Or, generate word cards from the CD-ROM.)

- Students can use their review list in a Word Play activity from a previous lesson, such as a word-find puzzle or a word criss-cross.

- Generate a practice activity from the CD-ROM.

Posttest Have students carefully tear out the posttest form on Student Book page 104. Students should pair up with their buddies or partners and exchange School Lists (page 101 in the Student Book). Students take turns testing each other on their respective spelling words. Collect the posttest sheets and score them. Mastery is 10 out of 12, or 80%. For students who do not achieve posttest mastery, see page xv in this Teacher's Edition.

Lesson 27

Past Tense. Add *-ed* to most verbs to form the past tense. Some words require a spelling change (*drop e, y to i*).

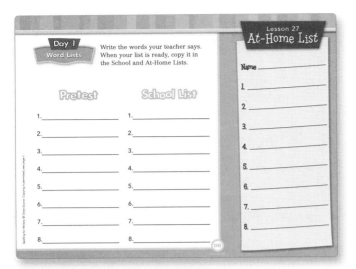

Before Photocopy the Answer Key/ Shopping List page (page 131 in this Teacher's Edition) for each student.

During Say each word in boldface, read the context sentence, and then repeat the word. Have students write the words in the Pretest column on page 105 of the Student Book.

After Distribute to students a copy of the Answer Key/Shopping List page so that they can correct their pretests.

- Students should cross out any misspelled words and write the correct spelling. Words that were correctly spelled can be replaced with words from the Shopping List. Assign the column from which students should choose their words. (See below.)

- Be sure that each student has a list of eight correctly spelled words, which they should copy into the School and At-Home Lists and the Sorting Boxes (page 131).

Pretest context sentences (spelling word in bold):

1. Please **try** to be quiet.
2. Yesterday, I **tried** to knit a scarf.
3. I **like** books about dogs.
4. I really **liked** that movie last night.
5. Now let's **talk** about fire safety.
6. A firefighter **talked** to the class yesterday.
7. Now **look** at the map on the wall.
8. My teacher **looked** happy this morning.

At-Home List Send the At-Home List home so that families can help their students study the words and features. Several literacy activities are given on the back of the At-Home List: writing present and past-tense words in different colors, creating a simple number code, finding letters in printed materials that spell words, and using letter tiles or magnetic letters to spell words.

NOTE The Shopping List provides words below grade level (column 1), words at grade level (column 2), and more challenging words that have the feature (column 3).

Name _____

Answer Key

1. try
2. tried
3. like
4. liked
5. talk
6. talked
7. look
8. looked

Shopping List

asked   parked   explored
cashed   chased   discovered
dusted   added   predicted
smiled   worked   estimated

Sorting Boxes

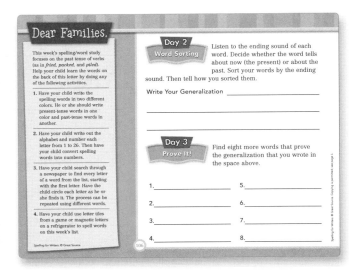

Have students look at the words carefully. Then have them decide for themselves a way or ways in which they can sort the words (do an open sort). Once they have made their sorts, ask them to say how the words are similar or different. What students say about the words shows you what they understand.

If students have not or cannot decide what the words have in common, model a way to sort all the words. You can use oversized word cards (CD-ROM) or a cut-up transparency (Transparency 23) and overhead to facilitate your model. Use the following Think Aloud with your visuals.

> **TEACHER'S THINK ALOUD** I notice that all my words mean that something is happening now (*try*) or has already happened (*tried*). All the words that mean something already happened end in *ed*. This is called the past tense. I can make one category of words that happen now and one category of words that happened in the past. My eye notices that some base words end with *y*, and I need to change the *y* to *i* before I add *ed*. In words that end in silent *e*, I need to drop the *e* and add *ed*. If we didn't drop the *e*, we would have *eed*, making the first *e* long. My ear also hears that sometimes *-ed* sounds like /d/ (*tried*) or /t/ (*looked*).

- Have students sort the words from their own lists. Circulate around the classroom and have each group or pair describe their method of sorting.

- Bring the class together to reach a consensus about the generalization. An example is this: *We add -ed to make words show the past tense.* Have students write their version on page 106 of the Student Book.

- Remind students that they have to remember not only to add *–ed* to make some past-tense words, but they also have to remember to make spelling changes. The spelling changes are similar to the ones they have learned about when adding *–es* to make a plural (Lesson 22).

- You might also write the generalization on a sentence strip or poster to display for the duration of the lesson. Leave room for students to add some of their Prove It! words from Day 3.

- Students can preserve their word sorts by gluing the word cards to a separate sheet of paper. Otherwise, they can store their Sorting Boxes. (See page xi in this Teacher's Edition.)

Day 3
Prove It!

Have students review the generalization and find more examples in available readable materials, such as storybooks, rhyming books, or labeled picture books. Be sure students can read the words that they find, and that the words prove the generalization. For example, you may wish to point out that some words, such as *see/saw,* show past tense without adding -*ed*. You may want to adjust the number of words students should find, depending on students' needs. Invite students to share their lists with the class. Keep these lists in a class word bank or chart for future reference.

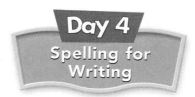

Day 4
Spelling for Writing

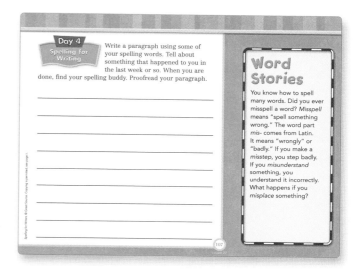

Point out that a narrative is a story that may or may not be true. Have students first think about something that they took part in or that happened to them. Remind them to think of an event that will allow them to use several spelling words. Offer these tips about writing a narrative:

- The events are usually told in the order in which they happened.

- Words such as *first, then,* and *after* show time order.

- Focus on just one event so that the narrative is clear and interesting.

Proofreading Tip Ask students to explain the difference between reading and proof-reading. Emphasize the care that must be taken when proofreading. Then, use a large piece of text to demonstrate how to touch every word with a finger or pencil so that the eyes concentrate on one word at a time.

Word Stories Tell students that a prefix is a word part. It is added to the beginning of some words. A prefix changes the meaning of a word. Explain that *mis-* is a prefix. Ask students what *misplace* might mean ("put in the wrong place"). Then discuss the meanings of other words, such as *misuse, misprint,* and *mispronounce.*

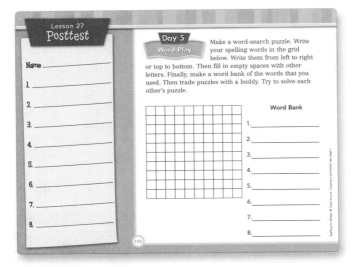

If possible, display a word-search puzzle for students to see as a model. Suggest that students first write their spelling words in the puzzle. Then, when they fill in the empty spaces afterwards, they may wish to use many of the same letters that appeared in their words. This makes the puzzles harder to solve. Remind students to fill in the Word Bank before they exchange puzzles.

Posttest Have students tear out the perforated posttest. Students should pair up with their buddies or partners and exchange School Lists (page 105 in the Student Book). Students take turns testing each other on their respective spelling words. Collect the posttest sheets, score them, and record the correct response percentages (Teacher's Edition page 180). Mastery is 6 out of 8 words correct (75%). For students who do not achieve posttest mastery, see page xv in this Teacher's Edition.

Anchor Words After the posttest, have students select one or two anchor words to help them remember the word feature in this lesson. Record the words on the "Anchor Words" poster and refer to them in the Review lesson.

Lesson 28

Past Tense. Add -ed to most verbs to form the past tense, even though the letters represent three different sounds (*needed, played, walked*).

Day 1
Pretest and Word Lists

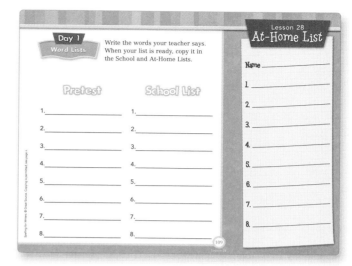

Before Photocopy the Answer Key/ Shopping List page (page 136 in this Teacher's Edition) for each student.

During Say each word in boldface, read the context sentence, and then repeat the word. Have students write the words in the Pretest column on page 109 of the Student Book.

After Distribute to students a copy of the Answer Key/Shopping List page so that they can correct their pretests.

- Students should cross out any misspelled words and write the correct spelling. Words that were correctly spelled can be replaced with words from the Shopping List. Assign a column from which students should choose their words. (See below.)

- Be sure that each student has a list of eight correctly spelled words, which they should copy into the School and At-Home Lists and the Sorting Boxes (page 136).

Pretest context sentences (spelling word in bold):

1. I *played* checkers with my sister.
2. I *needed* a pencil, so my teacher let me use his.
3. I *walked* home with two friends.
4. Last Saturday it *rained*, so our game was cancelled.
5. I really *wanted* to win that contest!
6. My father *helped* me find my shoes.
7. Our new puppy came when I *called* it.
8. The farmer *planted* corn, beans, and tomatoes.

At-Home List Send the At-Home List home so that families can help their students study the words and features. Several literacy activities are given on the back of the At-Home List: finding regular past-tense verbs and classifying the sound, making scrambled word puzzles, playing "Memory" with spelling words, and alphabetizing words.

> **NOTE** The Shopping List provides words below grade level (column 1), words at grade level (column 2), and more challenging regular past-tense verbs (column 3).

Name _____

Shopping List

hated	hunted	scrubbed
looked	kissed	snacked
filled	trained	lived
handed	tried	rented

Sorting Boxes

Day 2
Word Sorting

Have students look at the words carefully. Then have them decide for themselves a way or ways in which they can sort the words (do an open sort). Once they have made their sorts, ask them to say how the words are similar or different. What students say about the words shows you what they understand.

If students have not or cannot decide what the words have in common, model a way to sort all the words. You can use oversized word cards (CD-ROM) or a cut-up transparency (Transparency 24) and overhead to facilitate your model. Use the following Think Aloud with your visuals.

Dear Families,

This week's spelling/word study focuses on the different sounds that *-ed* can stand for in past-tense words (as in *waited*, *stayed*, and *missed*). Help your child learn the words on the back of this letter by doing any of the following activities.

1. Have your child search newspapers and magazines for words that end in *-ed*. Read the words aloud and have your child tell if the word ending sounds like that in *waited*, *stayed*, or *missed*.

2. Write the present- and past-tense forms of words on small pieces of paper. Place them face down and play "Memory." Each person takes a turn turning over two slips at once. When a person turns over slips showing different forms of the same word, that person keeps the pair. If the words are different, both are returned to their face-down position.

3. Have students list their words in alphabetical order.

Spelling for Writers. © Great Source.

Day 2
Word Sorting

Listen to the ending sound in each word. Sort your words by the way the endings sound. Then explain how you sorted them into groups.

Write Your Generalization _____

_____

Day 3
Prove It!

Find eight more words that prove the generalization that you wrote in the space above.

1. _____   5. _____
2. _____   6. _____
3. _____   7. _____
4. _____   8. _____

> **TEACHER'S THINK ALOUD** I know I need to use my brain, ears, and eyes when I read these cards. All of my spelling cards have something in common. I notice that all my words mean past tense so they all end in *ed*. However, I hear that sometimes *ed* sounds like /ed/ as in *planted*, sometimes like /d/ as in *played*, and sometimes like /t/ as in *liked*.

- Have students sort the words from their own lists. Circulate around the classroom and have each group or pair describe their method of sorting.

- Bring the class together to reach a consensus about the generalization. An example is this: *The* ed *ending can make three different sounds, even though the spelling is the same.* Have students write their version on page 110 of the Student Book.

- If appropriate for your students, point out that when *-ed* adds a syllable to a word, then it is pronounced /ĕd/. If not, the letters are pronounced as /d/ or /t/.

- You might also write the generalization on a sentence strip or poster to display for the duration of the lesson. Leave room for students to add some of their Prove It! words from Day 3.

- Students can preserve their word sorts by gluing the word cards to a separate sheet of paper. Otherwise, they can store their Sorting Boxes. (See page xi in this Teacher's Edition.)

Have students review the generalization and find more examples in available reading matter, such as social studies books, storybooks, science books, or other readable materials. Be sure students can read the words that they find and that the words prove the generalization. You may want to adjust the number of words students should find, depending on students' needs. Invite students to share their lists with the class. Keep these lists in a class word bank or chart for future reference.

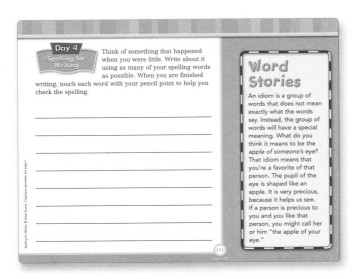

Students are asked to write a personal narrative about something that happened when they were little. The goal of the assignment is for students to use their spelling words in a piece of writing, so encourage them to use as many words as possible from their spelling and Prove It! lists. Also watch students' use of other past-tense verbs so that you can judge whether they have internalized the generalization.

Offer these tips for writing:

- A narrative usually tells events in the order in which they happened.

- Words such as *when, then*, and *next* show time order.

- Focus on one event to keep the writing clear and interesting.

- Use some dialogue to add interest.

Proofreading Tip Demonstrate for the students how to touch every letter with a pencil to make sure that all the letters are correct and none were left out.

Word Stories Tell students that people use idioms all the time. Idioms are groups of words that taken together have a special meaning. Offer a few suggestions, such as "I am going to *keep an eye on* this," or "Don't make *a big deal* out of it." Discuss reasons why idioms can be hard for people to understand if English is not their first language. Then ask students if they have ever heard the expression "You're the apple of my eye." Have students look at each other's pupils and explain why they are like apples (round). Explain that something precious has great value. Ask students to name things that are precious, such as family or jewels. Then invite students to identify people or pets that are the apples of their eyes.

Word Play and Posttest

Display the telephone keypad, drawing attention to the correspondence between numerals and letters. Demonstrate how students can identify *rained* from 724-6330. Ask a volunteer to identify the letters that correspond to the numeral 4 in item 2 (G,H,I). Then have students complete the activity alone or in pairs. If students find the activity too challenging, list the answers randomly on the board or refer students to the Answer Key page so that they can work from a list of words.

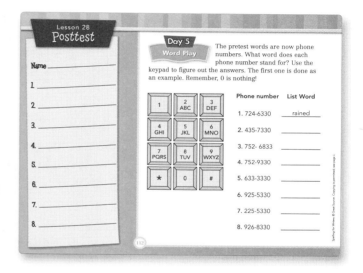

Answers

1. rained	5. needed
2. helped	6. walked
3. planted	7. called
4. played	8. wanted

Posttest Have students tear out the perforated posttest. Students should pair up with their buddies or partners and exchange School Lists (page 109 in the Student Book). Students take turns testing each other on their respective spelling words. Collect the posttest sheets, score them, and record the correct response percentages (Teacher's Edition page 180). Mastery is 6 out of 8 words correct (75%). For students who do not achieve posttest mastery, see page xv in this Teacher's Edition.

Anchor Words After the posttest, have students select one or two anchor words to help them remember the word feature in this lesson. Record the words on the "Anchor Words" poster and refer to them in the Review lesson.

Lesson 29 Preconsonant Nasals.
The letter *n* is a nasal consonant. When it comes before another consonant, it is called a preconsonant nasal and it is hard to hear (*long*).

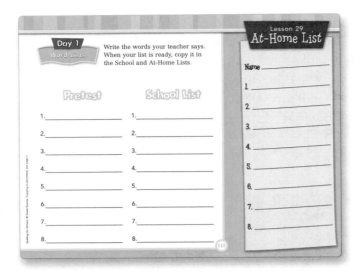

Day 1
Pretest and Word Lists

Before Photocopy the Answer Key/ Shopping List page (page 141 in this Teacher's Edition) for each student.

During Say each word in boldface, read the context sentence, and then repeat the word. Have students write the words in the Pretest column on page 113 of the Student Book.

After Distribute to students a copy of the Answer Key/Shopping List page so that they can correct their pretests.

- Students should cross out any misspelled words and write the correct spelling. Words that were correctly spelled can be replaced with words from the Shopping List. Assign the column from which students should choose their words. (See below.)

- Be sure that each student has a list of eight correctly spelled words, which they should copy into the School and At-Home Lists and the Sorting Boxes (page 141).

Pretest context sentences (spelling word in bold):

1. I must **find** my library book today.
2. I can **sing** that whole song.
3. This animal lives both on **land** and in water.
4. **Thank** you for driving me home.
5. I will **bring** juice to the soccer game.
6. That dog has a **long** tail.
7. The plant will **bend** toward the light.
8. Let me **think** for a minute and I will remember the address.

At-Home List Send the At-Home List home so that families can help their students study the words and features. Several literacy activities are given on the back of the At-Home List: making words, rhyming words, and making up riddles.

NOTE The Shopping List provides words below grade level (column 1), words at grade level (column 2), and more challenging words that have the feature (column 3).

Name _____

Answer Key

1. find	**5.** bring
2. sing	**6.** long
3. land	**7.** bend
4. thank	**8.** think

Shopping List

pink	wink	belong
sink	stand	clank
hang	strong	blond
hand	wrong	skunk

Sorting Boxes

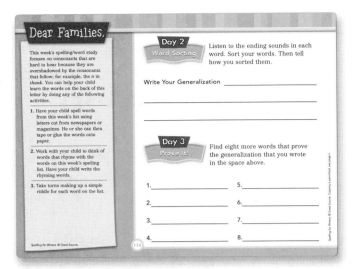

Day 2
Word Sorting

Have students look at the words carefully. Then have them decide for themselves a way or ways in which they can sort the words (do an open sort). Once they have made their sorts, ask them to say how the words are similar or different. What students say about the words shows you what they understand.

If students have not or cannot decide what the words have in common, model a way to sort all the words. You can use over-sized word cards (CD-ROM) or a cut-up transparency (Transparency 25) and overhead to facilitate your model. Use the following Think Aloud with your visuals.

TEACHER'S THINK ALOUD When I look at my words, I notice that they end with *n* and another consonant. The other consonant is either *d*, *g*, or *k* as in *bend*, *sing*, or *think*. When I say my words out loud, I notice that the *n* is hard to hear, so I will have to be very careful to include the *n* when I write these words.

- Have students sort the words from their own lists. Circulate around the classroom and have each group or pair describe their method of sorting.

- Bring the class together to reach a consensus about the generalization. Example: *The* n *is hard to hear in words that end with* nd, ng, *or* nk. Have students write their version on page 114 of the Student Book.

- Tell students that writers sometimes leave the *n* out of words such as *thank* and *find* because it is hard to hear. Remind them to use their brain, ears, and eyes when they spell such words.

- You might also write the generalization on a sentence strip or poster to display for the duration of the lesson. Leave room for students to add some of their Prove It! words from Day 3.

- Students can preserve their word sorts by gluing the word cards to a separate sheet of paper. Otherwise, they can store their Sorting Boxes. (See page xi in this Teacher's Edition.)

Day 3
Prove It!

Have students review the generalization and find more examples in available reading materials, such as textbooks, storybooks, puzzle books, or other appropriate texts. Be sure students can read the words that they find and that the words prove the generalization. You may want to adjust the number of words students should find, depending on students' needs. Invite students to share their lists with the class. Keep these lists in a class word bank or chart for future reference.

Day 4
Spelling for Writing

Remind students that expository writing gives information about something real. Tell students that now they have a chance to tell something about their own city or state. Talk with students about the kinds of details that they could include in their writing. Make a list for them to use when they write. Students should use as many spelling words and Prove It! words as they can.

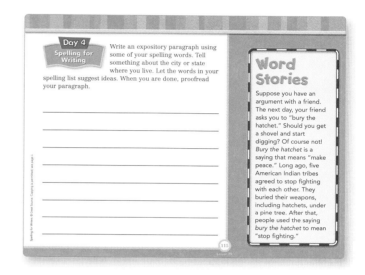

Day 4
Spelling for Writing

Write an expository paragraph using some of your spelling words. Tell something about the city or state where you live. Let the words in your spelling list suggest ideas. When you are done, proofread your paragraph.

Word Stories

Suppose you have an argument with a friend. The next day, your friend asks you to "bury the hatchet." Should you get a shovel and start digging? Of course not! *Bury the hatchet* is a saying that means "make peace." Long ago, five American Indian tribes agreed to stop fighting with each other. They buried their weapons, including hatchets, under a pine tree. After that, people used the saying *bury the hatchet* to mean "stop fighting."

Offer these tips about writing an expository paragraph:

- Make a list of details you want to include.

- Use the most interesting details.

- The first sentence will introduce the topic; the last sentence will bring the writing to a close.

Proofreading Tip Remind students how to use a paper marker under each line so the eyes concentrate on one line at a time.

Word Stories Students may be interested to know that the five American Indian tribes who first "buried the hatchet" in the late 1600s were the Mohawk, Oneida, Onondaga, Cayuga, and Seneca. Together, these groups became known as the Iroquois Nation or the Five Nations. After the Tuscarora joined in 1722, the group was called the Six Nations. The constitution of the Iroquois Nation was called the Great Law of Peace. Benjamin Franklin was so impressed with the Iroquois constitution that he suggested its use as a model for the new constitution of the United States.

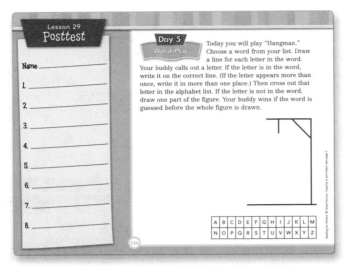

Demonstrate for students how to play "Hangman." Choose a word from this lesson, such as *thank*. Draw a frame on the board and write five blanks below it. Have students take turns guessing letters. Write correct choices on the blanks. Draw part of the stick figure for incorrect choices. Draw them in this order: head, body, eye, mouth. Explain that students will try to guess all the letters before the drawing is completed. If they do, they get to choose the next word. If they do not, you get to select a second word.

Posttest Have students tear out the perforated posttest. Students should pair up with their buddies or partners and exchange School Lists (page 113 in the Student Book). Students take turns testing each other on their respective spelling words. Collect the posttest sheets, score them, and record the correct response percentages (Teacher's Edition page 180). Mastery is 6 out of 8 words correct (75%). For students who do not achieve posttest mastery, see page xv in this Teacher's Edition.

Anchor Words After the posttest, have students select one or two anchor words to help them remember the word feature in this lesson. Record the words on the "Anchor Words" poster and refer to them in the Review lesson.

Periodically, check writing samples from your students for transfer of the word features that have been taught. The features for the last three lessons are as follows:

Lesson 27: Past Tense
Lesson 28: Past Tense
Lesson 29: Preconsonant Nasals

Lesson 30 Short and Long *a* (multisyllabic words). The words all have more than one syllable and at least one short *a* or long *a* vowel phoneme (*cannot, baseball*).

Day 1
Pretest and Word Lists

Before Photocopy the Answer Key/ Shopping List page (page 146 in this Teacher's Edition) for each student.

During Say each word in boldface, read the context sentence, and then repeat the word. Have students write the words in the Pretest column on page 117 of the Student Book.

After Distribute to students a copy of the Answer Key/Shopping List page so that they can correct their pretests.

- Students should cross out any misspelled words and write the correct spelling. Words that were correctly spelled can be replaced with words from the Shopping List. Assign the column from which students should choose their words. (See below.)

- Be sure that each student has a list of eight correctly spelled words, which they should copy into the School and At-Home Lists and the Sorting Boxes (page 146).

Pretest context sentences (spelling word in bold):

1. My **backpack** is heavy because it's full of books.
2. The caterpillar **became** a butterfly.
3. I **cannot** stay up late on school nights.
4. The month of **April** has thirty days.
5. That **grapevine** has been growing for years.
6. My favorite sport is **baseball**.
7. Everyone became quiet after the movie **began**.
8. My **grandmother** lives in Ohio.

At-Home List Send the At-Home List home so that families can help their students study the words and features. Several literacy activities are given on the back of the At-Home List: writing words using letters cut from newspapers and magazines, hunting for shorter words within long words, illustrating words, and making up riddles for words.

NOTE The Shopping List provides words below grade level (column 1), words at grade level (column 2), and more challenging multisyllable words with the feature (column 3).

Name _____

Shopping List
_____

classes   having   attach
grabbed   chapter   rabbit
mailbox   painful   await
railroad   trailer   toenail

Sorting Boxes

Day 2
Word Sorting

Have students look at the words carefully. Then have them decide for themselves a way or ways in which they can sort the words (do an open sort). Once they have made their sorts, ask them to say how the words are similar or different. What students say about the words shows you what they understand.

If students have not or cannot decide what the words have in common, model a way to sort all the words. You can use oversized word cards (CD-ROM) or a cut-up transparency (Transparency 26) and overhead to facilitate your model. Use the following Think Aloud with your visuals.

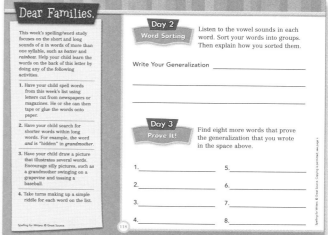

TEACHER'S THINK ALOUD I can see that my words are all a little bit long. When I say my words out loud, I notice that they have more than one vowel sound. I know that a word has as many syllables as it has vowel sounds. In other words, there is one vowel sound in each syllable. The word *grapevine* has two vowel sounds, therefore it has two syllables. So I need to be careful when I sort my words because I see many vowel letters in some words, but I only want to listen to the vowel sounds. When I listen to the vowel sounds, I hear that each word has either the short vowel *a* sound or the long vowel *a* sound, as in *backpack* and *became*.

- After students work on their own, bring the class together to reach a consensus about the generalization. An example is this: *Each of my words has a short* a *sound in one of the syllables or a long* a *sound in one of the syllables.* Have students write their version on page 118 of the Student Book.

- Point out that everything students have learned before about short and long *a* in one-syllable words holds true in syllables within multisyllable words. For example, the letter pattern in *grape* works within the longer word *grapevine*.

- Some students might also notice another category of words: compound words. Those students might want to sort their words again. This time, they will have one category of compound words and one category of the other words.

- You might write the generalization on a sentence strip or poster to display for the duration of the lesson. Leave room for students to add some of their Prove It! words from Day 3.

- Students can preserve their word sorts by gluing the word cards to a separate sheet of paper. Otherwise, they can store their Sorting Boxes. (See page xi in this Teacher's Edition.)

Have students review the generalization and find
more examples in available reading materials,
such as magazines, catalogs, calendars, or other
appropriate materials. Be sure students can read
the words that they find, and that their words

prove the generalization. You may want to adjust the number of words students should
find, depending on students' needs. Invite students to share their lists with the class.
Keep these lists in a class word bank or chart for future reference.

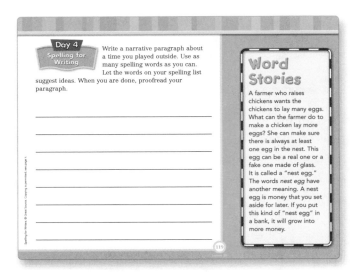

Students are asked to write a narrative
about a time they played outside. Tell
them to let their spelling words and
Prove It! words suggest what, exactly,
to write about. The purpose of the
assignment is to see how well students
can use their spelling words and apply
the generalization.

- A narrative should focus on one event.

- The words on the list can influence what to write about.

- A narrative has a beginning, a middle, and an end.

- Use some dialogue to make the narrative interesting.

Proofreading Tip Tell students that careful proofreaders know that they sometimes
make mistakes. They learn what those mistakes are and make a special effort to check
their writing for those errors. Have students think of an error they tend to make. For
example, do they tend to leave the *e* marker off the ends of words or syllables? Suggest
that they do a special pass through their writing to check for that error.

Word Stories Make sure students understand the analogy between the nest egg that induces a chicken to lay more eggs and the nest egg that people put in the bank. The financial kind of nest egg grows because banks pay interest. Each month, the bank adds a little money to the total. You might also ask if students are familiar with other idioms involving nests. For example, an "empty nest" is a family whose children have grown up and moved away. To "feather one's nest" means to increase one's wealth and live more comfortably. This expression refers to some birds' habit of lining their nests with feathers to create a soft place for their eggs.

Day 5
Word Play and Posttest

Ask volunteers to tell what word scrambles are. If students do not know, demonstrate by scrambling the letters of a familiar word. Then explain that students are going to make their own word scrambles today using spelling words. Show students where the scrambled words go on the page. When students have created the rest of the word scrambles, have them swap pages with a spelling buddy and try to solve each other's word scrambles. Students might find it easier to work with cut-apart letter cards, which can be found on pages 189–190 of this Teacher's Edition.

Lesson 30
Posttest

Name _____
1. _____
2. _____
3. _____
4. _____
5. _____
6. _____
7. _____
8. _____

Day 5
Word Play

Play "Mix It Up and Pass It On!" Take the letters of each spelling word and mix them up. Then write the mixed-up letters of each word in the left column. Trade your word scrambles with a buddy. Your buddy should write the words in the right column.

Mix It Up!   **Pass It On!**
1. _____   1. _____
2. _____   2. _____
3. _____   3. _____
4. _____   4. _____
5. _____   5. _____
6. _____   6. _____
7. _____   7. _____
8. _____   8. _____

Posttest Have students tear out the perforated posttest. Students should pair up with their buddies or partners and exchange School Lists (page 117 in the Student Book). Students take turns testing each other on their respective spelling words. Collect the posttest sheets, score them, and record the correct response percentages (Teacher's Edition page 180). Mastery is 6 out of 8 words correct (75%). For students who do not achieve posttest mastery, see page xv in this Teacher's Edition.

Anchor Words After the posttest, have students select one or two anchor words to help them remember the word feature in this lesson. Record the words on the "Anchor Words" poster and refer to them in the Review lesson.

Lesson 31 — Short and Long e (multisyllabic words).
The words all have more than one syllable and at least one short e or long e vowel phoneme (*pencil, even*).

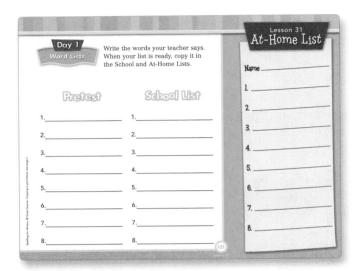

Before Photocopy the Answer Key/Shopping List page (page 151 in this Teacher's Edition) for each student.

During Say each word in boldface, read the context sentence, and then repeat the word. Have students write the words in the Pretest column on page 121 of the Student Book.

After Distribute to students a copy of the Answer Key/Shopping List page so that they can correct their pretests.

- Students should cross out any misspelled words and write the correct spelling. Words that were correctly spelled can be replaced with words from the Shopping List. Assign a column from which students should choose their words. (See below.)

- Be sure that each student has a list of eight correctly spelled words, which they should copy into the School and At-Home Lists and the Sorting Boxes (page 151).

Pretest context sentences (spelling word in bold):

1. I do my homework in my **bedroom**.
2. Is the number an odd number or an **even** number?
3. I need to sharpen this **pencil**.
4. The **teacher** read the name of every student.
5. The last month of the year is **December**.
6. Thanksgiving always falls in **November**.
7. I can't have a pet cat **because** I'm allergic to cats.
8. I'm **reading** a wonderful book.

At-Home List   Send the At-Home List home so that families can help their students study the words and features. Several literacy activities are given on the back of the At-Home List: writing words using different colors for different vowel sounds, writing words so that they cross at a letter they have in common, and spelling words with letter tiles or letter cards.

> **NOTE** The Shopping List provides words below grade level (column 1), words at grade level (column 2), and more challenging multisyllable words with the feature (column 3).

Name _____

<table>
<tr><td colspan="2">

Answer Key

1. bedroom   5. December

2. even   6. November

3. pencil   7. because

4. teacher   8. reading

</td><td colspan="3">

Shopping List

ended	better	benches
enter	everything	fresher
easy	clearing	beaten
meaning	easily	cheated

</td></tr>
</table>

Sorting Boxes

Have students look at the words carefully. Then have them decide for themselves a way or ways in which they can sort the words (do an open sort). Once they have made their sorts, ask them to say how the words are similar or different. What students say about the words shows you what they understand.

If students have not or cannot decide what the words have in common, model a way to sort all the words. You can use oversized word cards (CD-ROM) or a cut-up transparency (Transparency 27) and overhead to facilitate your model. Use the following Think Aloud with your visuals.

> **TEACHER'S THINK ALOUD** These words are a little bit long, like the ones from last week. I notice that all my words have more than one vowel sound. I know that a word has as many syllables as it has vowel sounds. In other words, there is one vowel sound in each syllable. The word *even* has two vowel sounds; therefore, it has two syllables. So I need to be careful when I sort my words because I see many vowel letters in some words, but I only want to listen to the vowel sounds. When I listen to the vowel sounds, I hear that the word has either the short *e* sound or the long *e* sound, as in *pencil* and *December*.

- Have students sort the words from their own lists. Circulate around the classroom and have each group or pair describe their method of sorting.

- Bring the class together to reach a consensus about the generalization. Example: *I sorted my words and I discovered that each word has a short* e *sound in one of the syllables or a long* e *sound in one of the syllables.* Have students write their version on page 122 of the Student Book.

- Point out that everything students have learned before about short and long *e* in one-syllable words holds true in syllables within multisyllable words. For example, the letter pattern in *pen* works within the longer word *pencil*.

- You might also write the generalization on a sentence strip or poster to display for the duration of the lesson. Leave room for students to add some of their Prove It! words from Day 3.

- Students can preserve their word sorts by gluing the word cards to a separate sheet of paper. Otherwise, they can store their Sorting Boxes. (See page xi in this Teacher's Edition.)

Day 3
Prove It!

Have students review the generalization and find more examples in available reading materials, such as calendars, catalogs, storybooks, or other appropriate materials. Be sure students can read the words that they find and that their words prove the generalization. You may want to adjust the number of words students should find, depending on students' needs. Invite students to share their lists with the class. Keep these lists in a class word bank or chart for future reference.

Day 4
Spelling for Writing

Students will write a paragraph about themselves. Pose questions similar to the ones on page 123 of the Student Book to help students choose a narrow focus to write about. Tell them to use as many spelling words and Prove It! words as possible. Offer these tips on writing about themselves:

- Write about something that is different from what you think someone else will write about.

- Present the details in an order that makes sense, for example, time order.

- Start each sentence with different words.

Proofreading Tip Instruct the students to read their writing aloud to make sure that no words were left out and that the sentences sound smooth and clear.

Word Stories Clipped words are shortened forms of longer words. They enter the English language as their usage becomes at least as common as their longer predecessors. Ask students what clipped words come from these longer words:

limousine (*limo*)   caravan (*van*)   tuxedo (*tux*)

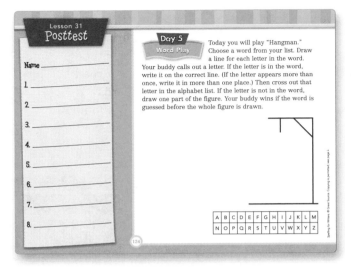

Demonstrate for students how to play "Hangman." Choose a word from this lesson, such as *pencil*. Draw a frame on the board and write six blanks below it. Have students take turns guessing letters. Write correct choices on the blanks. Draw part of the stick figure for incorrect choices. Draw them in this order: head, body, arm, arm, leg, leg. Explain that students will try to guess all the letters before the drawing is completed. If they do, they get to choose the next word. If they do not, you get to select a second word.

Posttest Have students tear out the perforated posttest. Students should pair up with their buddies or partners and exchange School Lists (page 121 in the Student Book). Students take turns testing each other on their respective spelling words. Collect the posttest sheets, score them, and record the correct response percentages (Teacher's Edition page 180). Mastery is 6 out of 8 words correct (75%). For students who do not achieve posttest mastery, see page xv in this Teacher's Edition.

Anchor Words After the posttest, have students select one or two anchor words to help them remember the word feature in this lesson. Record the words on the "Anchor Words" poster and refer to them in the Review lesson.

Lesson 32

Short and Long _i_ (multisyllabic words). The words all have more than one syllable and at least one short _i_ or long _i_ vowel phoneme (_dinner, tiger_).

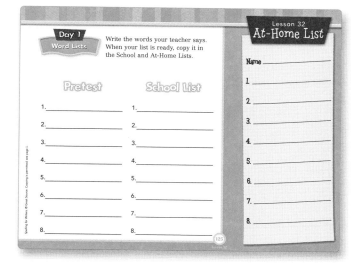

Day 1
Pretest and Word Lists

Before Photocopy the Answer Key/Shopping List page (page 156 in this Teacher's Edition) for each student.

During Say each boldfaced word, read the context sentence, and then repeat the word. Have students write the words in the Pretest column on page 125 of the Student Books.

After Give each student a copy of the Answer Key/Shopping List page to correct the pretest.

- Students should cross out misspelled words and replace them with the correct spellings. Words that were spelled correctly can be replaced with words from the Shopping List. Assign a column from which students should choose their words (See the note below).

- Check to see that each student ends up with a list of eight correctly spelled words, which they should copy into the School and At-Home Lists and the Sorting Boxes (page 156).

Pretest context sentences (spelling word in bold):

1. We ate **dinner** at 6:30.
2. You can ride your bike on the **sidewalk** but not in the road.
3. Yes, our old dog is still **alive** and well.
4. I always check **prices** before I buy something.
5. You can tell a **tiger** by the stripes in its fur.
6. We all laughed at the **silly** joke.
7. Did you hear **something** outside?
8. A large shoe had made a **footprint** in the soft earth.

At-Home List Send the At-Home List home so that families can use the following activities with their children; word hunt, scrambled words puzzles, hidden words.

> **NOTE** The Shopping List provides words below grade level (column 1), at grade level (column 2), and above grade level with the feature (column 3).

Name _____

Answer Key

1. dinner
2. sidewalk
3. alive
4. prices
5. tiger
6. silly
7. something
8. footprint

Shopping List

spinning   singing   picture

himself   wishes   simple

wider   driveway   sliding

nicer   timeline   mighty

Sorting Boxes

Have students look at the words carefully. Then have them decide for themselves a way or ways in which they can sort the words (do an open sort). Once they have made their sorts, ask them to say how the words are similar or different. What students say about the words shows you what they understand.

If students have not or cannot decide what the words have in common, model a way to sort all the words. You can use oversized word cards (CD-ROM) or a cut-up transparency (Transparency 28) and overhead to facilitate your model. Use the following Think Aloud with your visuals.

Dear Families,

This week's spelling/word study focuses on the short and long sounds of *i* in words with more than one syllable. Help your child learn about short vowels by learning the words on the back of this letter and by doing any of the following activities.

1. Go on a word hunt with your child. Together, scan words in print around you, such as newspapers, magazines, advertisements, and signs. Collect multisyllabic words with the sound of short *i* and long *i*. Use your child's list as a guide.

2. Help your child make scrambled word puzzles for you to solve. Show him or her how to scramble the letters of each word and list the scrambled words in one column. Next to each word, the child should draw lines for you to write on. See how many of the words you can unscramble and write on the lines.

3. Have your child draw a picture and try to hide a spelling word somewhere in it.

Day 2 Word Sorting Listen to the vowel sounds in each word. Sort your words. Then tell how you sorted them.

Write Your Generalization _____

Day 3 Prove It! Find eight more words that prove the generalization that you wrote in the space above.

1._____   5._____
2._____   6._____
3._____   7._____
4._____   8._____

TEACHER'S THINK ALOUD Like the words last week and the week before, I notice that all my words have more than one vowel sound. I know that a word has as many syllables as it has vowel sounds. In other words, there is one vowel sound in each syllable. The word *sidewalk* has two vowel sounds, therefore it has two syllables. So I need to be careful when I sort my words because I see many vowel letters in some words, but I only want to listen to the vowel sounds. When I listen to the vowel sounds, I hear that the word has either the short vowel *i* sound, or the long vowel *i* sound, as in *silly* and *alive*.

- Have students sort the words from their own lists. Circulate around the classroom and have each group or pair describe their method of sorting.

- Bring the class together to reach a consensus about the generalization, for example: *I sorted my words and I discovered that each word has a short* i *sound in one of the syllables or a long* i *sound in one of the syllables.* Have students write their version on page 126 of the Student Book.

- Point out that everything students have learned before about short and long *i* in one-syllable words holds true in syllables within multisyllable words. For example, the letter pattern in *side* works within the longer word *sidewalk*.

- You might write the generalization on a sentence strip or poster to display for the duration of the lesson. Leave room for students to add some of their Prove It! words from Day 3.

- Students can preserve their word sorts by gluing the word cards to a separate sheet of paper. Otherwise, they can store their Sorting Boxes. (See page xi in this Teacher's Edition.)

Have students review the generalization and find more examples in available reading materials, such as storybooks, poetry books, newspapers, or other appropriate materials. Be sure students can read the words that they find and that their words prove the generalization. You may want to adjust the number of words students should find, depending on students' needs. Invite students to share their lists with the class. Keep these lists in a class word bank or chart for future reference.

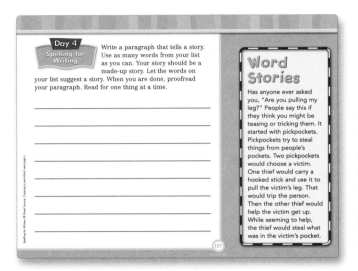

Tell students that today they will use their words to write a narrative paragraph. A narrative tells a story, usually in the order the events happened. Have them read their words and think about characters or settings that the words bring to mind. Offer these tips on writing a story:

- Use a graphic organizer to plan your story (beginning, middle, end).

- A story has characters and a setting.

- Use dialogue to add interest.

Proofreading Tip Explain to students that it is hard to focus on too many things at one time when proofreading. Tell them that good editors focus on just one thing when they check someone's writing. Students should go through their writing several times.

Word Stories Remind students that people often use expressions that do not mean exactly what they say. One such expression is *to pull someone's leg.* Explain its meaning: "to fool or trick someone." Like many other expressions, this one had a very different meaning long ago. Explain, if necessary, what pickpockets are and how they usually operate. Then discuss that a *victim* is someone whom the pickpockets decide to rob. Have students compare and contrast the old and new meanings of *pulling someone's leg.*

Day 5
Word Play and Posttest

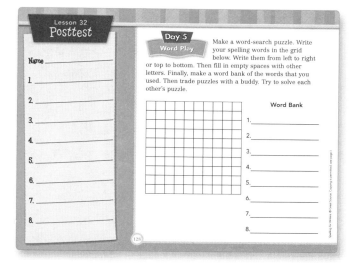

If possible, display a word-search puzzle for students to see as a model. Suggest that students first write their spelling words in the puzzle. Then, when they fill in the empty spaces afterwards, they may wish to use many of the same letters that appeared in their words. This makes the puzzles harder to solve. Remind students to fill in the Word Bank before they exchange puzzles.

Posttest Have students tear out the perforated posttest. Students should pair up with their buddies or partners and exchange School Lists (page 125 in the Student Book). Students take turns testing each other on their respective spelling words. Collect the posttest sheets, score them, and record the correct response percentages (Teacher's Edition page 180). Mastery is 6 out of 8 words correct (75%). For students who do not achieve posttest mastery, see page xv in this Teacher's Edition.

Anchor Words After the posttest, have students select one or two anchor words to help them remember the word feature in this lesson. Record the words on the "Anchor Words" poster and refer to them in the Review lesson.

Periodically, check writing samples from your students for transfer of the word features that have been taught. The features for the last three lessons are as follows:

Lesson 30: Short and Long *a* (multisyllabic words)
Lesson 31: Short and Long *e* (multisyllabic words)
Lesson 32: Short and Long *i* (multisyllabic words)

Lesson 33 — Short and Long *o* (multisyllabic words).

The words all have more than one syllable and at least one short *o* or long *o* vowel phoneme (*rocket, awoke*).

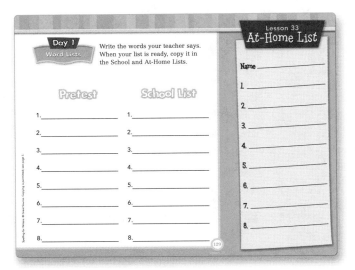

Before Photocopy the Answer Key/ Shopping List page (page 161 in this Teacher's Edition) for each student.

During Say each boldfaced word, read the context sentence, and then repeat the word. Have students write the words in the Pretest column on page 129 of the Student Book.

After Give each student a copy of the Answer Key/Shopping List page to correct the pretest.

- Students should cross out misspelled words and replace them with the correct spellings. Words that were spelled correctly can be replaced with words from the Shopping List. Assign a column from which students should choose their words (see the note below).

- Check to see that each student ends up with a list of eight correctly spelled words, which they should copy into the School and At-Home Lists and the Sorting Boxes (page 161).

Pretest context sentences (spelling word in bold):

1. Please hang your coat in the **closet.**
2. You need a key to **unlock** this door.
3. The playground has swings and a **sandbox.**
4. We watched the **rocket** head into space.
5. People in **olden** times traveled by horse.
6. The **rodeo** started with a parade of riders.
7. Everyone **awoke** to the sound of thunder.
8. Three of the kittens have pink **noses.**

At-Home List Send the At-Home List home so that families can use the following activities with their children: alphabetical order, making words, and rhyming words.

> **NOTE** The Shopping List provides words below grade level (column 1), at grade level (column 2), and above grade level with the feature (column 3).

Name _____

Shopping List

boxes	rocker	oddball
jogger	softest	beyond
only	oatmeal	voter
over	joker	broken

Sorting Boxes

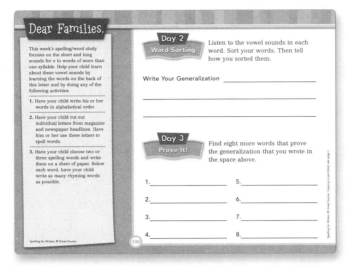

Day 2 — Word Sorting

Have students look at the words carefully. Then have them decide for themselves a way or ways in which they can sort the words (do an open sort). Once they have made their sorts, ask them to say how the words are similar or different. What students say about the words shows you what they understand.

If students have not or cannot decide what the words have in common, model a way to sort all the words. You can use oversized word cards (CD-ROM) or a cut-up transparency (Transparency 29) and overhead to facilitate your model. Use the following Think Aloud with your visuals.

> **TEACHER'S THINK ALOUD** When I read my words aloud, I notice that they have more than one vowel sound. I know that a word has as many syllables as it has vowel sounds. In other words, there is one vowel sound in each syllable. The word *sandbox* has two vowel sounds; therefore, it has two syllables. So I need to be careful when I sort my words because I see many vowel letters in some words, but I only want to listen to the vowel sounds. When I listen to the vowel sounds, I hear that the word has either the short *o* sound or the long *o* sound, as in *rocket* and *noses*.

- Have students sort the words from their own lists. Circulate around the classroom and have each group or pair describe their method of sorting.

- Bring the class together to reach a consensus about the generalization. Example: *I sorted my words and I discovered that each word has a short* o *sound in one of the syllables or a long* o *sound in one of the syllables.* Have students write their version on page 130 of the Student Book.

- Point out that everything students have learned before about short and long *o* in one-syllable words holds true in syllables within multisyllable words. For example, the letter pattern in *lock* works within the longer word *unlock*.

- You might also write the generalization on a sentence strip or poster to display for the duration of the lesson. Leave room for students to add some of their Prove It! words from Day 3.

- Students can preserve their word sorts by gluing the word cards to a separate sheet of paper. Otherwise, they can store their Sorting Boxes. (See page xi in this Teacher's Edition.)

Day 3

Prove It!

Have students review the generalization and find more examples in available reading materials, such as nonfiction books, storybooks, magazines, or other appropriate materials. Adjust the reading material and the number of words students should find, as appropriate. Be sure students can read the words that they find and that their words prove the generalization. You may want to adjust the number of words students should find, depending on students' needs. Invite students to share their lists with the class. Keep these lists in a class word bank or chart for future reference.

Day 4

Spelling for Writing

Students are asked to list words that fit categories that relate to some of the Pretest words. If students need ideas, do one or more of the categories as a whole-group activity.

Sample answers:

Things you can unlock: a car trunk, a door, a suitcase

Things you might find in a sandbox: a pail, a shovel, a toy truck

Things you might find in a closet: clothing, shoes, towels

Things you might see at a rodeo: cattle, cowboy hats, rope

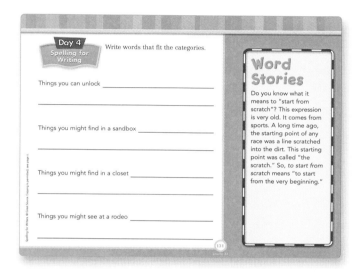

Proofreading Tip Students probably know about one or two errors they make consistently. They should make a separate pass through their writing looking specifically for each error.

Word Stories Remind students that people often use expressions that do not mean exactly what they say. One such expression is "starting from scratch." Ask if students have heard the expression before. If they have, discuss the context. Explain that starting from scratch not only means starting at the beginning but also starting from basics. Give the example of baking something either from scratch or from a mix; items baked from scratch start with basic ingredients, as opposed to ones that have already been combined. You may wish to point out that *scratch* is also used to mean "money." In this sense, it means something that has to be scratched for, just as a chicken scratches for food.

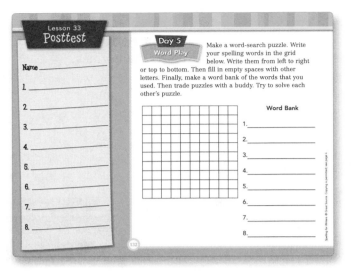

Day 5
Word Play and Posttest

If possible, display a word-search puzzle for students to see as a model. Suggest that students first write their spelling words in the puzzle. Then, when they fill in the empty spaces afterwards, they may wish to use many of the same letters that appeared in their words. This makes the puzzles harder to solve. Remind students to fill in the Word Bank before they exchange puzzles.

Posttest Have students tear out the perforated posttest. Students should pair up with their buddies or partners and exchange School Lists (page 129 in the Student Book). Students take turns testing each other on their respective spelling words. Collect the posttest sheets, score them, and record the correct response percentages (Teacher's Edition page 180). Mastery is 6 out of 8 words correct (75%). For students who do not achieve posttest mastery, see page xv in this Teacher's Edition.

Anchor Words After the posttest, have students select one or two anchor words to help them remember the word feature in this lesson. Record the words on the "Anchor Words" poster and refer to them in the Review lesson.

Lesson 34

Short and Long _u_ (multisyllabic words). The words all have more than one syllable and at least one short _u_ or long _u_ vowel phoneme (_funny, useful_).

Day 1
Pretest and Word Lists

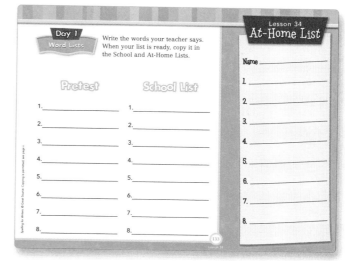

Before Photocopy the Answer Key/Shopping List page (page 166 in this Teacher's Edition) for each student.

During Say each boldfaced word, read the context sentence, and then repeat the word. Have students write the words in the Pretest column on page 133 of the Student Book.

After Give each student a copy of the Answer Key/Shopping List page to self-correct the pretest.

- Students should cross out misspelled words and replace them with the correct spellings. Words that were spelled correctly can be replaced with words from the Shopping List. Assign a column from which students should choose their words (see the note below).

- Check to see that each student ends up with a list of eight correctly spelled words, which they should copy into the School and At-Home lists and the Sorting Boxes (page 166).

Pretest context sentences (spelling word in bold):

1. I like to give **useful** gifts, such as flashlights or dictionaries.
2. This kind of sticky tape has many **uses.**
3. I can stay here **until** dinnertime.
4. That **funny** cartoon made everyone laugh.
5. Your cat just crawled **under** the bed.
6. The company president has a **duty** to hold meetings.
7. Many stories begin with "Once **upon** a time."
8. This book cover became **unglued,** so I have to fix it.

At-Home List Send the At-Home List home so that families can use the following activities with their children: word hunt, word-search puzzles, and word chain.

> **NOTE** The Shopping List provides words below grade level (column 1), at grade level (column 2), and above grade level (column 3).

Name _____

Shopping List

puppy	number	until
buses	unhappy	bubble
user	confuse	usual
bluer	useless	uniform

Sorting Boxes

Have students look at the words carefully. Then have them decide for themselves a way or ways in which they can sort the words (do an open sort). Once they have made their sorts, ask them to say how the words are similar or different. What students say about the words shows you what they understand.

If students have not or cannot decide what the words have in common, model a way to sort all the words. You can use oversized word cards (CD-ROM) or a cut-up transparency (Transparency 30) and overhead to facilitate your model. Use the following Think Aloud with your visuals.

TEACHER'S THINK ALOUD When I read my words out loud, I notice that they have more than one vowel sound. I know that a word has as many syllables as it has vowel sounds. In other words, there is one vowel sound in each syllable. The word until has two vowel sounds; therefore, it has two syllables. So I need to be careful when I sort my words because I see many vowel letters in some words, but I only want to listen to the vowel sounds. When I listen to the vowel sounds, I hear that the word has either the short vowel *u* sound, or the long vowel *u* sound, as in *funny* and *duty*.

• Have students sort the words from their own lists. Circulate around the classroom and have each group or pair describe their method of sorting.

• Bring the class together to reach a consensus about the generalization. Example: *I sorted my words and I discovered that each word has a short* u *sound in one of the syllables, or a long* u *sound in one of the syllables.* Have students write their version on page 134 of the Student Book.

• Point out that everything students have learned before about short and long *u* in one-syllable words holds true in syllables within multisyllable words. For example, the letter pattern in *fun* works within the longer word *funny*.

• You might write the generalization on a sentence strip or poster to display for the duration of the lesson. Leave room for students to add some of their Prove It! words from Day 3.

• Students can preserve their word sorts by gluing the word cards to a separate sheet of paper. Otherwise, they can store their Sorting Boxes. (See page xi in this Teacher's Edition.)

Have students review their generalizations and find more examples in available reading materials, such as fairy tales, riddle books, craft books, or other appropriate materials. Adjust the number of words students should find, as appropriate. Be sure that students can read the words they find, and that their words prove the generalization. You may want to adjust the number of words students should find, depending on students' needs. Invite students to share their lists with the class. Keep these lists in a class word bank or chart for future reference.

Day 3
Prove It!

Day 4
Spelling for Writing

Day 4
Spelling for Writing
Write an expository paragraph that explains something. Use as many of your spelling words as you can. Your paragraph might tell what something does or how it works. It might tell how to do something. Let the words on your spelling list suggest topics. When you are done, proofread your paragraph.

Word Stories
Do you feel healthy, or are you feeling "under the weather"? The expression *under the weather* means "feeling sick." Long ago, many sailors thought that the weather made them sick. In fact, they were seasick. Bad weather made the ocean very rough. When sailors felt ill, they would go down below the deck of the ship. They would try to go "under the weather." Sailors who were under the weather were those who felt sick.

Tell students that they will use their words to write an expository paragraph. An expository paragraph explains something. Have students read their words and think about topics they might write about. You may wish to model this process by naming three words, such as *useful, uses,* and *unglued,* and then naming topics that the words bring to mind. For example, students might explain various uses for duct tape.

Proofreading Tip Explain that it is often easier to proofread someone else's writing because you are less familiar with it and less apt to skip over words. Have students proofread a partner's paper. Advise students to be respectful of other people's writing and only circle the errors.

Word Stories Remind students that idioms are groups of words that have a special meaning. Today, people say they are "under the weather" if they do not feel well. Ask students what might make someone feel under the weather. (colds, flu, earache) Explain that this expression once meant just what it said. Sick sailors would try to get "under the weather" by going down below the deck of the ship. They blamed the weather for making them feel sick. In fact, they were probably seasick. Seasickness is caused by motion and not by weather, but since the weather caused the seas to be rough, it seemed as if the weather caused the sailors' illness. You may wish to point out that many other expressions came from sailing ships. When we say someone "knows the ropes," we mean that the person knows how to do something. Sailing ships used to have many different ropes that raised and lowered different sails. Sailors who knew the ropes knew just which rope to grab to make the ship move a certain way.

Day 5
Word Play and Posttest

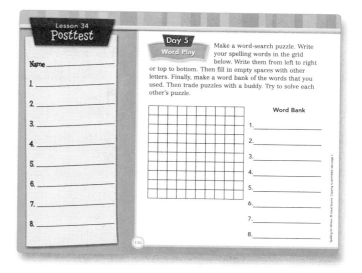

If possible, display a word-search puzzle for students to see as a model. Suggest that students first write their spelling words in the puzzle. Then, when they fill in the empty spaces afterwards, they may wish to use many of the same letters that appeared in their words. This makes the puzzles harder to solve. Remind students to fill in the Word Bank before they exchange puzzles.

Posttest Have students tear out the perforated posttest. Students should pair up with their buddies or partners and exchange School Lists (page 133 in the Student Book). Students take turns testing each other on their respective spelling words. Collect the posttest sheets, score them, and record the correct response percentages (Teacher's Edition page 180). Mastery is 6 out of 8 words correct (75%). For students who do not achieve posttest mastery, see page xv in this Teacher's Edition.

Anchor Words After the posttest, have students select one or two anchor words to help them remember the word feature in this lesson. Record the words on the "Anchor Words" poster and refer to them in the Review lesson.

Periodically, check writing samples from your students for transfer of the word features that have been taught. The features for the last two lessons are as follows:

Lesson 33: Short and Long *o* (multisyllabic words)
Lesson 34: Short and Long *u* (multisyllabic words)

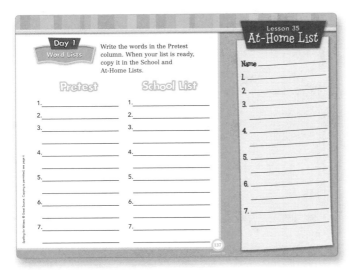

Day 1
Pretest and
Word Lists

Before There are three options for selecting the pretest words. Choose the one most appropriate for your students.

1. Have students think of words that fit the spelling patterns and write them.

2. Use the words that you and your class collected on the "Anchor Words" poster.

3. Use the examples given on page 171.

If you will dictate the words, either from the "Anchor Words" poster or from page 171, make an answer key by writing the words on a copy of Copy Master 1. Photocopy the filled-in answer key page for each student.

During Announce each word feature as listed on page 171. As you say each feature, also state the generalization and give the words or ask students to think of words. Students will write one or two words for each feature on page 137 of the Student Book.

After If you dictated words, distribute a copy of the answer key so that students can self-correct their pretests. Otherwise, correct students' pretests.

- For any word that students got correct, send them back to the lesson for that feature to select a word from their Prove It! List they want to learn to spell.

- Be sure that each student has a list of correctly spelled words, which they should copy into the School and At-Home Lists and the Sorting Boxes (use Copy Master 1 for the Sorting Boxes).

At-Home List Have students tear out the perforated At-Home List and take it home to use with families. Several literacy activities are given on the back of the At-Home List: playing oral word games, creating a word wall, and making up sentences using the initial letters of spelling words.

Word Features and Generalizations

1. **Past Tense.** Add -*ed* to most verbs to form the past tense, even though the letters represent three different sounds (*hiked*). (*Lessons 27, 28*)

2. **Preconsonant Nasals.** The letter *n* is a nasal consonant. When it comes before another consonant, it is called a preconsonant nasal and it is hard to hear (*long*). (*Lesson 29*)

3. **Short and Long Vowels (*a* in multisyllabic words).** The letter *a* can have a short sound or a long sound (*cannot, baseball*). (*Lesson 30*)

4. **Short and Long Vowels (*e* in multisyllabic words).** The letter *e* can have a short sound or a long sound (*pencil, even*). (*Lesson 31*)

5. **Short and Long Vowels (*i* in multisyllabic words).** The letter *i* can have a short sound or a long sound (*dinner, tiger*). (*Lesson 32*)

6. **Short and Long Vowels (*o* in multisyllabic words).** The letter *o* can have a short sound or a long sound (*rocket, awoke*). (*Lesson 33*)

7. **Short and Long Vowels (*u* in multisyllabic words).** The letter *u* can have a short sound or a long sound (*funny, useful*). (*Lesson 35*)

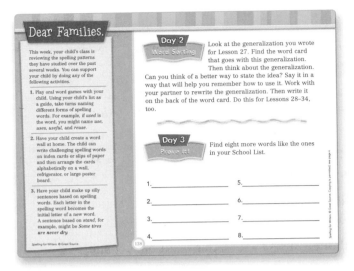

Day 2
Word Sorting

Look at the generalization you wrote for Lesson 27. Find the word card that goes with this generalization. Then think about the generalization. Can you think of a better way to state the idea? Say it in a way that will help you remember how to use it. Work with your partner to rewrite the generalization. Then write it on the back of the word card. Do this for Lessons 28–34, too.

Day 3
Prove It!

Find eight more words like the ones in your School List.

1. _____   5. _____
2. _____   6. _____
3. _____   7. _____
4. _____   8. _____

Day 2
Word Sorting

Today students will revisit the generalizations they wrote for Lessons 27–34. They will read them and then decide if they could be stated more clearly.

- Have students cut apart the Sorting Boxes to create word cards for this activity (Copy Master 1).

- Have them form pairs and turn to page 106 of their Student Books.

- Both students should read the generalization they wrote for Lesson 27 and identify the word cards that relate to this generalization. Then they should ask themselves if the generalization is clear. Could it be stated in a way that would be more helpful in remembering how to spell the words?

- You might work through the first generalization with the class to show students how to clarify and improve the wording.

- Students should then write the best version of the generalization on the back of a relevant word card and move on to the next generalization (Lesson 28).

As a closing step, have students work in pairs to sort their words into groups that make sense. Circulate through the room to talk with students about their word sorts. Students' explanations of their sorts tell you what they understand about how words work.

After students revisit and revise several generalizations for this lesson's review, send them off to find in readable materials more examples that prove as many of the generalizations as possible to be true. Provide appropriate reading materials,

Day 3
Prove It!

such as storybooks, poetry books, newspapers, and textbooks. Be sure that students can read the words they find and that their words prove each generalization. Adjust the amount and kind of reading material students will use as well as the number of words they should find, according to their needs. You might want to limit the scope of the word hunt by having some students search for words that prove only one or two of the generalizations.

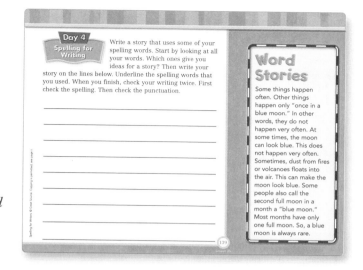

Day 4
Spelling for Writing

Encourage students to begin by working with partners to brainstorm story ideas. They might start by pairing nouns with past-tense verbs. Some combinations may suggest ideas for characters or situations. For example, the words *rabbit* and *wanted* might suggest a story about a rabbit that wanted a friend.

Offer these tips to students as they plan their stories:

- Write about just one event.

- Make sure the story has a clear beginning, middle, and end.

- Use some dialogue to bring some action to the story.

Proofreading Tip Remind students that a good proofreader checks a piece of writing for only one thing at a time. Although it can seem boring, it is important to make several passes through a piece of writing. For example, check the spelling the first time through and check the punctuation on the second pass.

Word Stories Tell students that our language contains many expressions that do not mean exactly what they say. One such expression is *once in a blue moon*. Ask if students have ever heard the expression. Discuss its meaning and ask for examples of when it might apply. For example, "once in a blue moon" someone finds hidden treasure. Ask volunteers to name other examples of events that rarely happen. You may wish to point out that many ancient people used full moons as a way of marking time. Often, the full moon at a particular time was named for an activity that happened at that time, such as the Harvest Moon, which is what people call the full moon that happens around harvest time in the fall. When there are two full moons within one calendar month, the second full moon is called the blue moon.

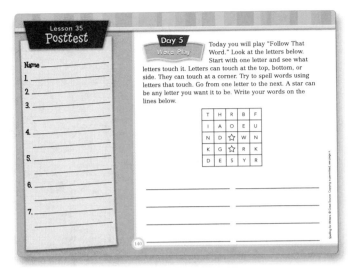

Lesson 35
Posttest

Name _____

1. _____
2. _____
3. _____
4. _____
5. _____
6. _____
7. _____

Day 5
Word Play

Today you will play "Follow That Word." Look at the letters below. Start with one letter and see what letters touch it. Letters can touch at the top, bottom, or side. They can touch at a corner. Try to spell words using letters that touch. Go from one letter to the next. A star can be any letter you want it to be. Write your words on the lines below.

T	H	R	B	F
I	A	O	E	U
N	D	☆	W	N
K	G	☆	R	K
D	E	S	Y	R

_____ _____
_____ _____
_____ _____
140 _____

Day 5
Word Play and Posttest

Tell students that they will play a game that requires them to look and to think. Review the directions on page 140 of the Student Book and make sure students understand that they can make many different words depending on the letters that they select. Demonstrate how student might find the word THANK, beginning with the letter T in the first row and then moving their finger to the right, down, diagonally down, and then straight down. Ask a volunteer to find some other word. Then have students complete the activity either independently or in pairs. After they have completed the activity, have them compare their answers.

Review Activities Other activities that students can do to review the words include the following:

- Have students choose a set of Sorting Boxes from a previous lesson and time themselves when they sort the cards. Students should sort them several times to see whether their sorting time gets faster. (Copy Masters of the pretest words can be found in the Transparencies and Copy Masters folder. Or, generate word cards from the CD-ROM.)

- Students can use their review list in a Word Play activity from a previous lesson, such as a word-search puzzle or a word criss-cross.

- Generate a practice activity from the CD-ROM.

Posttest Have students carefully tear out the posttest form on Student Book page 140. Students should pair up with their buddies or partners and exchange School Lists (page 137 in the Student Book). Students take turns testing each other on their respective spelling words. Collect the posttest sheets and score them. Mastery is 10 out of 12, or 80%. For students who do not achieve posttest mastery, see page xv in this Teacher's Edition.

Lesson 36 Benchmark Assessment.

Days 1-2
Word Lists

Days 1-2
Word Lists

Write the words your teacher says.

Benchmark Assessment

1._____	11._____
2._____	12._____
3._____	13._____
4._____	14._____
5._____	15._____
6._____	16._____
7._____	17._____
8._____	18._____
9._____	19._____
10._____	20._____

141

Dear Families,

This week your child will be given the last of three benchmark spelling assessments. Your child was given the same benchmark assessment at the beginning of the year and in the middle of the year. This assessment is a tool to gain insight into your child's current and developing knowledge about spelling. Information from the benchmark assessments allowed for classroom instruction that built on what your child already knew. Progress across the three benchmark assessments will inform next year's teacher about this year's growth.

Encourage your child to summarize and share with you whatever progress he or she has made this year. Remember that learning to spell is a process that develops over a period of years. Watch your child's writing as he or she continues to learn more about the English language, and you will see a stronger and stronger understanding of how words are spelled.

Before Have students locate page 141 in the Student Book on which they will record the spelling words. This benchmark assessment is the last of three opportunities for you to monitor each student's growth. There are no standards for mastery in the benchmark assessments. Rather, they are informative pieces for instructional planning.

During Say each word in boldface (page 176) aloud. The word features are identified in parentheses for your information. These words were specifically chosen because they represent grade-level words for a given feature. If you substituted other words Lesson 1, use them here. It is recommended that this assessment be administered over two to five days, in short intervals, in order to best meet the needs of your students and to avoid student fatigue. On Days 3-5, if the assessment is still ongoing, students can continue with the other activities after you administer a small portion of the assessment.

After Interpret students' responses, analyzing first their successes in spelling a word that meets the word feature criterion and then taking a hard look at where they may have miscued, perhaps recalling a different word feature and misapplying it. We strongly encourage you to analyze students' responses not for errors but for insights into the strategies that students employed to spell each word.

We suggest you do not mark in the Student Book. A record sheet is provided (see page 179 in this Teacher's Edition). This records the features and allows you to document growth for each student. It is important for students not to see the markings, so simply transfer any attempts to the record sheet. Looking at the three Benchmark Assessments is your window into how students have progressed and what recommendations you might make to next year's teachers and to refine your own teaching.

Benchmark Assessment This is the last of three Benchmark Assessments. The Benchmark Assessments provide a record of students' spelling from this year and can be noted in a portfolio and passed along to next year's teachers.

1. **late** (short and long vowel *a*)
2. **yes** (short and long vowel *e*)
3. **big** (short and long vowel *i*)
4. **toe** (short and long vowel *o*)
5. **use** (short and long vowel *u*)
6. **try** (long vowel *y*)
7. **man** (short vowels *a, i*)
8. **mop** (short vowels *e, o*)
9. **dust** (short vowel *u*, long vowel *y*)
10. **keep** (long vowels *a, e, o*)
11. **ice** (long vowels *i, u*)
12. **child** (digraphs)
13. **free** (consonants blends)
14. **kick** (final consonants)

15. **stars** (plural -*s*)
16. **foxes** (plural -*es*)
17. **men** (irregular plurals)
18. **know** (silent consonant patterns)
19. **high** (silent vowel patterns)
20. **rain** (silent vowel patterns)
21. **told** (irregular past tense)
22. **wrapped** (past tense -*ed*)
23. **thank** (preconsonant nasals)
24. **apple** (short and long vowel *a*)
25. **letter** (short and long vowel *e*)
26. **inside** (short and long vowel *i*)
27. **opening** (short and long vowel *o*)
28. **cuter** (short and long vowel *u*)

Letter to the Families

Students may carefully remove the perforated section of page 141 in the Student Book and take it home to share with their families. It includes a note to families explaining the benchmark assessments and how they have been used to shape instruction. On the back of this note are several At-Home activities that families can use to support their students' learning. These activities include encouraging students to note similarities between words, writing frequent short notes to students, and playing word games.

Day 3
Delicious Words

After students have completed today's benchmark assessment, tell them that they are going to choose their favorite "delicious" words from the year. Use the collection of words on the "Delicious Words" poster to review words that students have discovered during the year. Ask students to share where they found the words, which words are their favorites, and which words they have used in their writing. Finally, have students look at their "delicious" words lists on Student Book pages 2 and 66 and the poster to identify their favorites. Have students list their favorite words on Student Book page 142 and challenge them to use as many of the words as they can in conversation today!

Day 4
Spelling for Writing

After students have completed today's benchmark assessment, review the instructions for the writing activity on page 143 of the Student Book. Explain that a list poem is a poem that lists thoughts about a subject. Read the example in the Student Book aloud. Have volunteers identify which sense each line appeals to. Briefly discuss other possible topics for poems. Then have students work

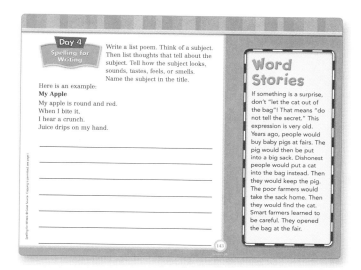

independently to write their own list poems. If time allows, ask volunteers to read their poems aloud.

Proofreading Tip Remind students that they should proofread everything they write. Ask them to list ways of proofreading that they use. Proofreading ideas include the following: touch a pencil point to each word or letter, read the writing aloud, ask a partner to check your writing, look for mistakes that you know you make often.

Word Stories On Student Book page 143, students are told that people often use expressions that do not mean exactly what they say. One such expression, or idiom, is *letting the cat out of the bag.* Ask if students have heard the expression before. If they have, discuss the context. Explain that *letting the cat out of the bag* means "letting a secret be known." Have students give examples of secrets that they might accidentally tell, such as a surprise party. On Student Book page 144, students are asked to find out what idioms are used in their homes.

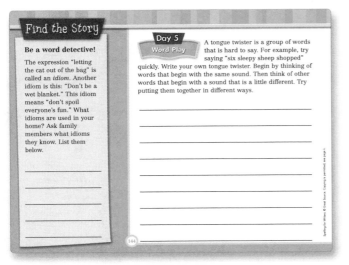

Day 5
Word Play

After students have completed today's benchmark assessment, have them turn to page 144 of the Student Book. Explain that a tongue twister is a phrase or sentence that is hard to say. Give an example, such as "Fat frogs flying fast" or "Three free throws." Encourage students first to work in pairs or small groups to discuss what makes a phrase hard to say. They can then work independently to write tongue twisters using these words.

Name_____ Grade_____

Benchmark Assessment Chart

Word and Feature	Lesson 1	Lesson 19	Lesson 36
1. **late** (short and long vowel *a*)			
2. **yes** (short and long vowel *e*)			
3. **big** (short and long vowel *i*)			
4. **toe** (short and long vowel *o*)			
5. **use** (short and long vowel *u*)			
6. **try** (long vowel *y*)			
7. **man** (short vowels *a*, *i*)			
8. **mop** (short vowels *e*, *o*)			
9. **dust** (short vowel *u*, long vowel *y*)			
10. **keep** (long vowels *a*, *e*, *o*)			
11. **ice** (long vowels *i*, *u*)			
12. **child** (digraphs)			
13. **free** (consonants blends)			
14. **kick** (final consonants)			
15. **stars** (plural -*s*)			
16. **foxes** (plural -*es*)			
17. **men** (irregular plurals)			
18. **know** (silent consonant patterns)			
19. **high** (silent vowel patterns)			
20. **rain** (silent vowel patterns)			
21. **told** (irregular past tense)			
22. **wrapped** (past tense -*ed*)			
23. **thank** (preconsonant nasals)			
24. **apple** (short and long vowel *a*)			
25. **letter** (short and long vowel *e*)			
26. **inside** (short and long vowel *i*)			
27. **opening** (short and long vowel *o*)			
28. **cuter** (short and long vowel *u*)			

Class Record Chart

Lesson

Student	2	3	4	5	6	7	9	10	11	12	13	14	15	18

Student	19	20	21	22	23	24	25	27	28	29	30	31	32	33	34

See the reteaching ideas on Teacher's Edition page xi for students who do not achieve 80% on the posttest.

Word Features and Generalizations in *Spelling for Writers*

Lesson 2: Short and Long a. A word spelled with a consonant-vowel-consonant (CVC) pattern usually has a short vowel sound (*cap*). A word spelled with a consonant-vowel-consonant-*e* (CVCe) pattern usually has a long vowel sound (*cape*).

Lesson 3: Short and Long e. The short e sound can be represented by *e* alone (*tell*). The long *e* sound can be represented by *ea* or *ee* (*heat, peel*).

Lesson 4: Short and Long i. A word spelled with a consonant-vowel-consonant (CVC) pattern usually has a short vowel sound (*fin*). A word spelled with a consonant-vowel-consonant-*e* (CVCe) pattern usually has a long vowel sound (*fine*).

Lesson 5: Short and Long o. A word spelled with a consonant-vowel-consonant (CVC) pattern usually has a short vowel sound (*hop*). A word spelled with a consonant-vowel-consonant-*e* (CVCe) pattern usually has a long vowel sound (*hope*).

Lesson 6: Short and Long u. A word spelled with a consonant-vowel-consonant (CVC) pattern usually has a short vowel sound (*tub*). A word spelled with a consonant-vowel-consonant-*e* (CVCe) pattern usually has a long vowel sound (*tube*).

Lesson 7: Long Vowels (final y). When a word ends with the sound of a long *a*, *e*, or *i*, it probably ends with the letter (*my*) or a vowel plus *y* (*play*).

Lesson 9: Short Vowels (a, i). A word spelled with a consonant-vowel-consonant (CVC) pattern usually has a short vowel sound (*bag, six*).

Lesson 10: Short Vowels (e, o). A word spelled with a consonant-vowel-consonant (CVC) pattern usually has a short vowel sound (*fox, ten*).

Lesson 11: Short and Long Vowels (u, y). The short *u* sound is represented by *u* in *sun*. The long sounds of *a*, *i*, and *e* can be represented by *y* or a vowel plus *y* (*way*).

Lesson 12: Long Vowels (silent letter patterns). Sometimes vowel letters make a pattern in which one vowel is long and one is silent, as in *rain*, *read*, and *road*.

Lesson 13: Long Vowels (i, u). The sound of long *i* can be represented by *i* alone (*find*), i plus the *e* marker (*life*), or *y* (*July*). The sound of long *u* can be represented by *u* alone or with *u* plus the *e* marker.

Lesson 14: Consonant Digraphs (ch, th). Two consonants can come together to make a single sound, as in *child*.

Lesson 15: Consonant Blends. When a consonant comes before *l* or *r*, the sounds are blended together (*free, blue*).

Lesson 18: Consonants (final *k, ck*). At the end of a word, the sound of /k/ can be represented by *k* or *ck*, as in *took* and *back*.

Lesson 19: Plurals (-*s*). Add –*s* to change most singular nouns into plural nouns (*girls*).

Lesson 20: Plurals (-*es*). Add –*es* to change singular nouns that end with *s, sh, ch*, and *x* into plural nouns (*lunches*).

Lesson 21: Plurals (-*s*, -*es*). Add –*s* to form the plural of most words. Add –*es* to words that end with *s, sh, ch*, and *x*.

Lesson 22: Plurals (*y* to *i*, irregular forms). When some words are changed to plurals, their spelling changes (*cries, children*).

Lesson 23: Consonants (silent letter patterns). Consonant letters can make a pattern in which one is silent, as in *knew* and *wrap*.

Lesson 24: Long Vowels (silent letter patterns). Sometimes letters make a pattern in which the vowel is long and one or more letters are silent, as in *yellow* and *night*.

Lesson 25: Long Vowels (silent letter patterns). Sometimes vowel letters make a pattern in which one vowel is long and one is silent, as in *sail* and *reach*.

Lesson 27: Past Tense. Add –*ed* to most verbs to form the past tense. Some words require a spelling change (drop *e*, *y* to *i*).

Lesson 28: Past Tense. Add –*ed* to most verbs to form the past tense, even though the letters represent three different sounds (*played, needed, walked*).

Lesson 29: Preconsonant Nasals. The letter *n* is a nasal consonant. When it comes before another consonant, it is called a preconsonant nasal and it is hard to hear (*long*).

Lesson 30: Short and Long Vowels (*a* in multisyllabic words). The words all have more than one syllable and a short *a* or long *a* vowel phoneme (*cannot, baseball*).

Lesson 31: Short and Long Vowels (*e* in multisyllabic words). The words all have more than one syllable and a short *e* or long *e* vowel phoneme (*pencil, even*).

Lesson 32: Short and Long Vowels (*i* in multisyllabic words). The words all have more than one syllable and a short *i* or long *i* vowel phoneme (*dinner, tiger*).

Lesson 33: Short and Long Vowels (*o* in multisyllabic words). The words all have more than one syllable and a short *o* or long *o* vowel phoneme (*rocket, awoke*).

Lesson 34: Short and Long Vowels (*u* in multisyllabic words). The words all have more than one syllable and a short *u* or long *u* vowel phoneme (*funny, useful*).

Spelling for Writers: Foundation in Research

Spelling for Writers is rooted in research that examines instructional methods and the developmental aspects of learning to spell. Spelling instruction has a long history in the United States. In the late 1700s, spellers were shipped from England or reprinted in America. The instructional method mimicked those used in England, where learning the alphabet and then combinations of letters prepared students to learn 180 syllables (Hodges, 1977). Learning to spell was followed by learning to read.

In 1839, Horace Mann claimed the whole word method was "the superior spelling method" (Hodges, 1977, p.4). He suggested utilizing a memorization approach (Hodges, 1977). The spelling bee became a popular activity in many communities.

In Joseph Rice's influential 1897 article, "The Futility of the Spelling Grind," an analysis of 33,000 U.S. students' spelling achievement was presented (Hodges, 1977). His work found that outside influences—such as age, home, or school environment—had little effect on achievement. Therefore, he recommended that students spend 15 minutes per day in spelling study, and the words studied should be carefully selected based on orthographic features and difficulty (Hodges, 1977). Rice's research shaped studies about spelling instruction into the next century. Then, in the 1950s, a new scientific inquiry called "linguistics" emerged. Linguists studied the English language and discovered that it was not as irregular as previously thought. This finding suggested that teaching students to understand the patterns and features of words would prove more powerful than memorization. However, spelling basals remained virtually unchanged – every student in a grade level got the same list of words to learn for the Friday test. Some basals attempted to provide for differentiation by having students that scored well on a pretest take additional "challenge" words. These students got more—not different— words to study.

While many linguists were constructing knowledge about the English language and figuring out how to best teach spelling, others focused on how students learn to spell. Read's (1971) landmark study of preschool children's invented spellings argued that their attempts were not random. Rather, he observed consistent and progressive changes in children's invented spellings over time. Relying on their operating knowledge of the language, the children's errors made sense. Beers and Henderson (1977) also found logical error patterns that changed both systematically and longitudinally (Henderson, 1987). This understanding of the developmental nature of how children learn to spell gradually began to inform classroom practice (Fresch, 2003, p.821).

Many researchers support the belief that spelling is a developmental process: All students progress through the same continuum, but some move along faster than others. Word and activity selection is suggested by such key educators as Cunningham and Hall (1994), Gentry (1981), Zutell (1996), Schlagal and Schlagal

(1992), and Bear, Invernezzi, Templeton and Johnston (2004). While these researchers suggest ways to meet the individual, developmental needs of students, much teacher organization and decision making is required to create instruction. *Spelling for Writers* uses the developmental research, the authors' direct work with students, and research on graded word lists to create a series that offers teachers an organized, research-based approach for meeting individual needs.

References

Bear, D., Invernizzi, M., Templeton, S., & Johnston, F. (2000). *Words their way: Word study for phonics, vocabulary, and spelling instruction* (2nd ed.). Upper Saddle River, NJ: Prentice Hall.

Beers, J. & Henderson, E. (1977). A study of developing orthographic concepts among first grade children. *Journal of Research in English, 11,* 133-148.

Cunningham, P. & Hall, D. (1994). *Making words: Multilevel, hands-on, developmentally appropriate spelling and phonics activities.* Parsippany, NJ: Good Apple.

Fresch, M.J. (2003). A national survey of spelling instruction: Investigating teachers' beliefs and practice. *Journal of Literacy Research,* 35, 819-848.

Gentry, R. (1981). Learning to spell developmentally. *The Reading Teacher*, 34, 378-381.

Henderson, E. (1987). *Learning to read and spell.* DeKalb, IL: Northern Illinois University Press.

Hodges, R.E. (1977). In Adam's fall: A brief history of spelling instruction in the United States. In H.A. Robinson (Ed.), *Reading and writing instruction in the United States: Historical trends* (pp.1-16). Newark, DE: International Reading Association.

Read, C. (1971). Pre-school children's knowledge of English phonology. *Harvard Educational Review,* 41, 1-34.

Schlagal, R.C. & Schlagal, J.H. (1992). The integral character of spelling: Teaching strategies for multiple purposes. *Language Arts*, 69, 418-424.

Templeton, S. (1983). Using the spelling/meaning connection to develop word knowledge in older students. *Journal of Reading*, 27, 8-14.

Zutell, J. (1996). The Directed Spelling Teaching Activity (DSTA): Providing an effective balance in word study instruction. *The Reading Teacher*, 50, 98-108.

Introducing *Spelling for Writers* to the Community

Open house is the perfect time to introduce *Spelling for Writers* to students' families and the larger community. By that time, the families will have received several letters from the first few lessons of the year. This is the teacher's opportunity to encourage families to support their student by reading the letter and trying to do some of the suggested activities. The families will see that they can still practice the words with their student, but now they have multiple ways to work with their children. Additionally, each letter provides ways for families to talk about more words than just what is on their list for the week.

At the Open House or other forum, engage families in a word-sorting activity. Few people can resist organizing a group of word cards left on the table! After families have sorted the cards, ask them to share how they grouped the words. The amount of word knowledge that is used while sorting words and sharing the results is key activity in *Spelling for Writers*.

Another Open House activity might be to tell the families that you would like them to think of how a word, such as *chauffeur*, is spelled. Ask them: *This is a word we hear and use but have rare occasion to write. What did you think about to spell the word?* They might have thought about the way the "sh" sound can be spelled, how the "r" at the end might be spelled since this is a person, and so on. They might have tried to visualize it. These are all aspects of being a good speller: Good spellers use what they know about the language and their past experiences with words. This is what *Spelling for Writers* aims to do, provide students with a number of dependable strategies for independent writing.

When families have personal experience with the program and understand its purpose and approach, they are more likely to work with their children to support their spelling growth.

Suggested Resources for Spelling and Word Study

Almond, J. (1985). *Dictionary of Word Origins*. Secaucus, NJ: Citadel Press.

Barnette, M. (1997). *Ladyfingers and Nun's Tummies*. NY: Vintage Books.

Bear, D., Templeton, S., Invernizzi, M. & Johnston, F. (2004). *Words Their Way: Word Study for Phonics, Vocabulary and Spelling Instruction* (third edition). Columbus: Merrill.

Blevins, W. (1998). *Phonics from A to Z*. NY: Scholastic.

Bolton, F. and D. Snowball (1993). *Teaching Spelling: A Practical Resource*. Portsmouth, NH: Heinemann.

Bolton, F. and D. Snowball (1993). *Teaching Spelling: A Practical Resource*. Portsmouth, NH: Heinemann.

Branreth, G. (1988). *The Word Book*. London: Robson Books.

Bryson, B. (1990). *The Mother Tongue*. New York: William Morrow and Company.

Cunningham, P. & Hall, D. (1994). *Making Words*. Parsippany, NJ: Good Apple, Inc.

Ericson, L. & Juliebö, M. (1998). *The Phonological Awareness Handbook for Kindergarten and Primary Teachers*. Newark, DE: International Reading Association.

Flavel, L & R. (1992). *Dictionary of Idioms*. London: Kyle Cathie Ltd.

Fresch, M. J. & Wheaton, A. (1997). Sort, search and discover: Spelling in the child-centered classroom. *The Reading Teacher*, 51, 20-31.

Fresch, M. J. & Wheaton, A. (2002). *Teaching and Assessing Spelling: A Practical Approach that Strikes the Balance Between Whole-Group and Individualized Instruction*. NY: Scholastic.

Fresch, M. J. & Wheaton, A. (2004). *The Spelling List and Word Study Resource Book*. NY: Scholastic.

Funk, W. (1950). *Word Origins*. New York: Wings Books.

Ganske, K. (2000). *Word Journeys*. NY: Guilford Press.

Gentry, J. R. (2004). *The Science of Spelling*. Portsmouth, NH: Heinemann.

Goodman, K. (1993). *Phonics Phacts*. Jefferson City, MO: Scholastic.

Hanson, J. (1972). *Homographs: Words That Look the Same*. Minneapolis, MN: Lerner Publications.

Henderson, E. (1990). *Teaching Spelling, 2nd Edition*. Boston: Houghton Mifflin.

Henderson, E. and Beers, J. W. (Eds.) (1980). *Developmental and Cognitive Aspects of Learning to Spell: A Reflection of Word Knowledge*. Newark, DE: International Reading Association.

Henry, M.A, (2003). *Effective Decoding and Spelling Instruction*. Baltimore, MD: Brookes.

Hoad, T. F. (1993). *Concise Oxford Dictionary of English Etymology*. New York: Oxford University Press.

Hodges, R. E. (1981). *Learning to Spell*. Urbana, IL: National Council of Teachers of English.

Hughes, M. & Searle, D. (1997). *The Violent E and Other Tricky Sounds: Learning to Spell from Kindergarten through Grade 6.* York, ME: Stenhouse.

Jones, C. F. (1999). *Eat Your Words: A Fascinating Look at the Language of Food.* Illustrated by J. O'Brien. NY: Delacorte Press.

Jones, C. F. (1991). *Mistakes That Worked.* NY: Doubleday.

Kennedy, J. (1996). *Word Stems: A Dictionary.* New York: Soho Press.

Lederer, R. (1990). *Crazy English.* New York: Pocket Books.

Powell, D. & Hornsby, D. (1993). *Learning Phonics and Spelling in a Whole Language Classroom.* Jefferson City, MO: Scholastic.

Merriam-Webster New Book of Word Histories. (1991). Springfield, MA: Merriam-Webster, Inc.

Room, A. (1986). *The Fascinating Origins of Everyday Words.* Chicago: NTC Publishing.

Shipley, J. (1945). *Dictionary of Word Origins* New York: Dorset Press.

Stowe, C. M. (1996). *Spelling Smart!* West Nyack, NY: Center for Applied Research in Education.

Terban, M. (1996). *Dictionary of Idioms.* NY: Scholastic.

Tompkins, G. and Yaden, D. (1986). *Answering Students' Questions about Words.* Urbana, IL: National Council of Teacher's of English

Traupman, J. C. (1995). *Latin and English Dictionary.* New York: Bantam Books.

Venezky, R. (1999). *The American Way of Spelling: The Structure and Origin of American English Orthography.* NY: Guilford Press.

Wagstaff, J. (1993). *Phonics That Work.* Jefferson City, MO: Scholastic.

White, R. (1994). *An Avalanche of Anoraks.* New York: Crown Trade Paperbacks.

Wilde, S. (1997). *What's a Schwa Sound Anyway? A Holistic Guide to Phonetics, Phonics, and Spelling.* Portsmouth, N.H.: Heinemann.

Young, S. (1994). *Rhyming Dictionary.* New York: Scholastic.

Zutell, J. (1996). The directed spelling teaching activity (DSTA): Providing an effective balance in word study instruction. *The Reading Teacher, 50, 98-108.*

a b c d e f

g h i j k l

m n o p q r

s t u v w x

y	z	a	a	e	e
i	i	o	o	u	u
b	d	g	l	m	n
p	r	s	s	t	t

Word List (grade 1) Boldfaced words are pretest words.

able	**brother**	dress	game
about	**bug**	**drink**	**gave**
am	**but**	each	**glue**
an	**can**	**eat**	goes
as	**cap**	egg	ham
ask	**cape**	even	**has**
at	**cash**	**fan**	**hat**
baby	**cat**	**fast**	hate
back	club	**fat**	**hid**
bag	**cold**	**father**	hide
ball	**crashing**	feel	**him**
bang	cutting	**fell**	**his**
bank	**dad**	**fill**	hit
been	**daddy**	filled	hold
beg	desk	fire	hole
began	**did**	fish	**hop**
bell	**dig**	fishing	**hope**
best	**dime**	**fit**	**hot**
big	**dish**	flag	huge
bit	**dock**	flap	**hush**
bite	**dog**	**flat**	**it**
blue	**dot**	flew	**junk**
bone	**drag**	fling	**just**
bother	drank	**flip**	**keep**
box	draw	**fog**	kind
bread	dream	**fun**	**lake**

last	not	run	spot
late	nut	rush	stall
left	other	sack	stand
leg	pan	sad	star
letter	pen	sale	start
lid	pick	sat	stink
lip	pill	sell	stop
little	pin	she	sum
lock	pine	sick	sun
log	pink	sing	sunk
long	pit	sink	tag
lost	plus	sip	tall
lot	pop	sit	tank
made	pot	slap	teeth
map	pretty	sled	tell
matter	pushing	sleep	ten
me	rabbit	slick	then
men	rag	slip	those
mice	rang	slop	tip
mom	rash	so	today
mother	reading	sock	told
mug	red	song	track
mush	ride	spell	trade
must	right	spill	train
name	ring	spin	trash
nice	rip	spine	truck
no	rug	spit	trunk

tune

use

wag

washing

we

when

white

wish

wishing

Word List (grade 2) Boldfaced words are pretest words.

added	**because**	book	cashed
aim	**bedroom**	**both**	cent
alive	bee	bow	chain
apples	**began**	**box**	changes
April	belong	**boxes**	chapter
as	below	**boy**	chase
ashes	benches	**boys**	chased
asleep	**bend**	brain	chat
at	better	branches	cheated
ate	beyond	brat	**cheek**
attach	**black**	**bright**	cheese
await	bleacher	bring	**chest**
awoke	blew	broken	**child**
babies	blind	brothers	**children**
back	**blink**	brushes	chin
backpack	**block**	bubble	cities
bag	blond	**bug**	clank
bags	blood	**bus**	classes
bark	bloom	buses	clay
baseball	blot	**bushes**	clean
bases	blow	but	clearing
bath	**blue**	**called**	**closet**
bathrooms	bluer	candies	coins
beat	blushes	**cannot**	colors
beaten	body	**cap**	confuse
became	bone	**cape**	**cook**

copies	dropped	**fine**	glue
countries	drove	fix	**goal**
crashes	drug	flashes	gone
cries	**duck**	flight	goodbye
crop	**ducks**	float	got
crow	due	fly	grabbed
cry	dusted	**footprint**	**grandmother**
cub	**duty**	**fox**	grape
cube	**each**	foxes	**grapevine**
cut	easily	frame	grow
cute	easy	**free**	grub
cuter	**eat**	freeze	guesses
day	enter	fresher	hail
days	estimated	Friday	hand
deal	**even**	**friend**	handed
December	ever	**friends**	hang
deer	everything	fright	has
dig	explored	frogs	**hat**
dime	eye	**from**	**hate**
dinner	fat	frown	having
discovered	**feel**	**fry**	hay
dishes	feet	**funny**	**heat**
dock	**fell**	gate	heated
dot	fight	gift	**help**
dress	filled	**girl**	**helped**
dresses	**fin**	**girls**	hid
driveway	**find**	glasses	**hide**

high	knapsack	losses	**needed**
himself	knead	**low**	net
hit	**knee**	luck	nice
hole	kneel	**lunch**	nicer
hop	**knew**	**lunches**	**night**
hope	knife	**mail**	**nod**
houses	**knot**	mailbox	**noses**
huge	**know**	main	**not**
hunted	knuckle	**man**	**November**
ice	lad	**many**	number
inch	ladies	mask	oat
inches	**land**	math	oatmeal
into	late	meaning	odd
itchy	leaf	**men**	oddball
jeans	leap	mice	**olden**
jogger	left	middle	on
joke	less	might	only
joker	lid	mighty	over
July	**life**	money	**pack**
June	lift	moose	**paid**
junk	**like**	**mop**	**pail**
just	**liked**	**mud**	pain
key	list	**mule**	painful
kid	lived	music	paint
kind	**long**	**my**	parked
kissed	**look**	myself	pat
kisses	**looked**	nap	pea

peach	railroad	**say**	skate
peaches	**rain**	**school**	**skies**
peel	**rained**	**schools**	skunk
pencil	raise	scrubbed	**sky**
penny	rashes	**sea**	sleep
pick	**reach**	seed	sleepy
picture	**read**	**set**	sliding
pin	**reading**	shape	slot
pine	rented	shock	smiled
pink	rest	shook	snacked
planes	rich	shot	snap
planted	riches	show	**snow**
play	**right**	shrub	softest
played	**road**	shut	**something**
plays	rocker	shy	songs
plus	**rocket**	**sick**	spell
pole	rode	**side**	**spot**
pot	**rodeo**	**sidewalk**	spray
pray	rooms	sigh	squares
predicted	**rope**	**sight**	stack
pretty	**row**	**silly**	stand
price	rude	simple	state
prices	rule	**sing**	stay
pride	**sail**	singing	stink
prize	sailboat	sink	strong
quick	**sandbox**	sisters	stuff
rabbit	**sat**	**six**	**sun**

sway	timeline	**used**	wreath
sweeter	toenail	**useful**	**wreck**
tail	**took**	useless	wrestle
talk	**top**	user	wring
talked	track	**uses**	wrinkle
tan	**trail**	usual	wrist
tap	trailer	**very**	**write**
tape	trained	vote	wrong
taxes	**traps**	voter	**wrote**
tea	trees	wagons	**yellow**
teacher	**tried**	**wait**	yes
team	tries	**walked**	**yet**
tell	trip	**wanted**	
ten	true	**way**	
thank	**try**	**went**	
that	**tub**	**wet**	
the	**tube**	when	
them	**tune**	**why**	
then	**under**	wider	
they	**unglued**	**win**	
thigh	unhappy	wink	
think	uniform	**wishes**	
thinking	**unlock**	**with**	
this	**until**	worked	
those	**upon**	worry	
throat	**us**	worth	
tiger	**use**	**wrap**	

Word List (grade 3) Boldfaced words are pretest words.

about	aquarium	bathroom	bland
absence	**are**	batted	blank
accident	**armies**	**batting**	blind
actors	army	beach	**blink**
afraid	around	beacon	**blue**
after	art	bead	boast
afternoon	ashes	beat	**boat**
age	ate	**became**	**boats**
aid	attic	**bedroom**	body
aide	attract	bees	boil
aim	aunt	beet	**book**
airmail	available	before	bookmark
airplane	avoid	begging	**bookstore**
allow	**away**	behave	bookworm
aloud	**babies**	**behind**	booties
already	back	**benches**	both
amaze	**background**	bend	**bottle**
amount	backpack	**berries**	bought
answer	backyard	beside	**bound**
ant	baked	**better**	boxes
anybody	bandage	**bigger**	boy
anyone	bark	**biggest**	**brace**
anything	**barn**	**birthday**	bracelet
anyway	baseball	birthmark	**brake**
applied	baseboard	**bite**	**brand**
appoint	bashful	blamed	brat

brave	**called**	chat	clay
bread	campfire	chatter	clean
break	campground	cheat	**cliffs**
breakthrough	**can't**	**check**	climb
breathe	candy	**cheek**	clipper
breeze	**cane**	**cheese**	**clock**
brick	canned	**chest**	closed
brief	**cannot**	**chick**	**cloud**
bright	cape	**chicks**	cloudy
bring	car	chief	clover
broil	cared	**children**	coach
broiled	caramel	chime	coal
brown	cases	chipping	coast
brush	cash	chips	**coat**
brushes	cashier	choice	coats
buffalo	caught	chopped	**coin**
buffet	**cent**	**chose**	**comb**
buggies	center	chubbier	**come**
bulge	**chain**	chunk	**comma**
bullies	**chair**	**church**	confuse
busier	**chairs**	**circle**	Congress
busy	**change**	circuit	control
butterfly	chapter	**cities**	cook
buzzer	charger	**city**	copper
cabins	charm	civic	**corn**
cage	chase	claim	**cost**
calf	chased	classes	**count**

counted	dare	downpour	earlier
courthouse	dark	downstairs	**earring**
cowboy	**darkest**	dozen	earthquake
cows	data	**drag**	**eastern**
cranky	**daytime**	dragged	easy
crashes	deaf	dragons	echo
cream	decade	**drank**	eggshell
create	deer	**draw**	eighty
creature	**delight**	**dream**	**ending**
cries	**desk**	**dress**	**enjoy**
croaking	**desks**	dressed	**eve**
crop	**destroy**	dribble	**even**
crowd	diaries	drift	everybody
crumb	**did**	drill	everything
crumble	dime	drink	everywhere
cry	dirty	dripping	exit
crybaby	disappoint	**drive**	eye
crying	disease	drive-in	**eyebrow**
cube	**dishes**	driveway	eye opener
cupid	ditch	dromedary	face
cute	**dock**	drooping	**faces**
cutest	dogs	drop	fairies
daddy	**door**	dropped	**faith**
dairies	doorstep	**drove**	**family**
daisy	**dotted**	due	fancier
danced	doubt	**dunk**	fancy
dances	down	each	**farm**

farther	flies	funnier	grab
fattest	**flight**	funny	grabbed
feast	flip	gain	graded
February	flipped	**gallon**	**grain**
feet	flirt	garage	**grandfather**
fence	**flock**	garden	**grandmother**
field	Florida	gasp	grape
fields	**flour**	geese	**graph**
fiend	**flower**	gem	graphics
finer	flu	**gentle**	gray
finest	fluid	get	greyhound
fingers	flute	**getting**	grief
finished	flutter	ghost	grinned
fir	fly	**giant**	**groan**
firefly	foil	**gift**	grounded
first	football	**gifts**	guess
fitted	footbridge	**girl**	**had**
fixed	for	give	**hailstorm**
flake	force	**given**	hair
flame	**forever**	glance	hairpin
flapping	found	**globe**	halfway
flashes	**fresh**	glossier	hands
flat	friend	**glue**	handsome
fled	fries	goal	**happiest**
flesh	frightened	goes	hare
flew	frost	gone	harm
flicker	fume	**goodbye**	hawk

hay	income	kneel	lightning
hear	**indoors**	**knew**	**liked**
heaviest	it's	**knife**	**limb**
heavy	its	knight	lined
heavyweight	jackknife	knit	listen
held	**January**	**knitted**	littlest
helpful	**jogger**	knob	**lived**
here	jogging	**knock**	load
hey	**join**	knot	loaf
hide	joined	**knotted**	loans
high	joint	knotting	locket
home	**joke**	**know**	lodge
homemade	joy	knuckle	logger
honest	**joyful**	labels	loudest
hooked	**July**	ladies	**loved**
hope	**June**	lady	loveliest
hopped	jungle	**laid**	luckier
hopping	junk	lamb	lunch
horse	just	lay	lunches
horsefly	kept	lead	madder
hotter	**kick**	leak	**made**
hottest	**kidded**	leash	mail
hound	**kind**	**leashes**	mailed
hugged	kisses	left	male
I	knapsack	lender	mankind
ignored	knead	**lifted**	**mask**
inches	**knee**	light	matter

meanwhile	**needed**	or	**phase**
men	nephew	orange	**phone**
mend	**new**	ouch	phony
met	newscast	our	photo
mice	**next**	**out**	physical
mighty	**nicest**	**outside**	picked
mink	niece	owe	**piece**
mist	night	**owned**	pinch
mixed	nightgown	pack	pink
mixing	nineties	**page**	piped
modern	**no**	paint	**place**
money	**nobody**	**pancake**	plan
monkey	noise	**part**	**plane**
moodier	**noontime**	party	**planned**
moose	not	passed	play
mopped	notches	past	played
more	note	pastries	player
moth	noted	**patted**	playground
mouth	numb	**patting**	playing
much	**number**	payday	plea
mug	**oak**	peace	**please**
mule	**oath**	peaked	pluck
multiplied	**oatmeal**	penknife	plugged
music	obey	**pennies**	**plum**
mustard	**oil**	**people**	**plus**
myself	olive	percent	**point**
nastiest	one	**phantom**	policeman

pond	quality	**red**	rubies
poor	quart	redder	rude
popped	quarterback	reddest	rummage
posies	queen	**redo**	**runner**
pounce	question	**reed**	runway
pour	**quick**	**refill**	**sadder**
praise	quiet	**remind**	**safer**
precook	quill	renew	**sail**
precut	**quilt**	repay	**sailboat**
predawn	quit	rephrase	**sale**
prefix	quite	**reply**	sample
preheat	**quiz**	research	**sank**
premature	quote	restful	**save**
premix	raced	restore	scar
preset	**rack**	retell	scent
pretest	**railroad**	return	scored
preview	rain	**review**	scowl
price	rainier	rich	screams
priest	rainy	riches	scribes
print	raisin	**right**	sea
prize	rank	ripe	seacoast
problem	**read**	road	seam
punch	**reading**	road	search
puppies	**ready**	**robber**	seasick
puppy	**really**	robbing	seat
push	**recall**	rock	see
quack	recopy	rubbing	**seem**

seesaw	six	sobbed	**stab**
send	skies	**soft**	**stage**
sent	skinnier	some	**stair**
shack	skinny	somebody	stairwell
shape	skipped	**someday**	**stamp**
share	**skips**	someone	**star**
shark	**skunk**	sometime	stare
sheep	skyward	**somewhere**	stared
shell	slammed	son	starring
shipped	sleep	sounded	start
shoe	**slice**	**space**	stay
shook	slid	spaced	step
shopped	sloped	speaker	stepping
shortcut	slot	speaking	**still**
shortening	slunk	speeding	stinkiest
shot	smallest	speedway	stir
shower	smash	spell	stirring
shriek	**smiled**	spend	stock
shrink	**smiles**	sphere	**stone**
shy	**smock**	spies	**stopped**
sick	**smoke**	spoil	stork
sigh	smooth	spoke	stormy
sight	snack	**spotted**	**story**
sillier	snail	spray	straight
silliest	**snap**	**sprung**	strait
sir	**sneak**	**squeak**	**strange**
sister	**snowy**	squeeze	strap

stray	their	told	unable
stream	them	tomb	unclean
street	these	tombstone	under
strength	they	took	understand
stretch	they're	toothpick	undo
struck	thick	toy	undone
stunk	thicken	trade	uneven
sum	thief	trap	unfit
sun	thigh	trapped	unhappy
sunlight	thimble	trend	unhook
sunshine	think	tried	unkind
survey	third	trophies	unknown
sway	this	trophy	unlock
swimming	those	tropics	unscramble
tabby	threw	true	unselfish
tail	through	trunk	unstable
tale	thumb	trust	untangle
taller	thumbnail	truthful	unzip
tallest	Thursday	try	upset
tank	tight	tube	us
tape	time	tune	use
taught	timid	tuned	usher
teacher	tipped	twenty	value
team	tired	twice	vote
teeth	to	two	voted
tender	today	typewriter	waist
than	together	ugly	wait

war

warehouse

warm

was

washer

waved

wax

way

weak

wear

week

weekend

weigh

went

were

west

whack

whale

what

what's

wheat

wheel

wheelchair

when

whenever

where

which

while

whip

whistle

white

whole

why

windstorm

wink

with

without

womb

women

won

word

work

worry

wrap

wrapping

wreath

wreck

wren

wrench

wrestle

wriggle

wring

wrinkle

wrist

wristwatch

write

writer

writers

writing

written

wrong

wrote

yield

you're

your

youth